Suspicion and Silence:
The Right to Silence in Criminal Investigations

Edited by

David Morgan

and

Geoffrey M. Stephenson

BLACKSTONE
PRESS LIMITED

First published in Great Britain 1994 by Blackstone Press Limited,
9–15 Aldine Street, London W12 8AW. Telephone: 081-740 1173

ISBN: 1 85431 380 0

British Library Cataloguing in Publication Data
A CIP catalogue record for this book is available from the British Library.

Typeset by Montage Studios Ltd, Tonbridge, Kent
Printed by Ashford Colour Press, Gosport, Hampshire

Contents

Contents

Preface

With one exception, the papers in this collection were presented to a conference organised by the Institute for Social Research at the University of Kent to mark the publication in December 1993 of the government's Criminal Justice and Public Order Bill (House of Commons Bill 9 Session 1993/94). The Bill includes provisions to restrict a defendant's right to silence in response to police questioning and in the courts. Supporters of this change argue that the right to silence is an anachronistic impediment to justice and its abolition would lead to the conviction of more guilty offenders in the courts. However, there is growing concern that removal of this age-old right will expose suspects to greater pressures from the police and increase the risks of false confessions and miscarriages of justice. This was the position taken by the Royal Commission on Criminal Justice (1993) in recommending that the right to silence should be retained.

As the book went to press the government's proposed restrictions on the right of silence had been approved in both Houses of Parliament. However, during the Committee stage in the House of Lords on 23 May, Earl Ferrers for the government said that consideration would be given to the need for further amendments. The book went to press before the Report stage in the House of Lords. Experts predicted that, if there were any late government amendment, it would go no further than to provide that adverse inferences could not be drawn from silence before a caution — and that on balance it seemed less rather than more likely that the government would move such an amendment.

The key issues raised by the debate are considered in the following chapters in relation to recent evidence on the conduct of criminal investigations by the police. Much of the evidence discussed here — in chapters by Roger Leng, Michael Maguire, Stephen Moston and Geoffrey M. Stephenson, John Baldwin, Roger Evans and Gisli Gudjonsson — was prepared for the Royal Commission and informed the Commission's recommendations. The book concludes with chapters by Tom Williamson, a senior police officer involved in recent changes in police interviewing training, Adrian Zuckerman, an authority on criminal evidence, who was unfortunately unable to attend the conference last December, and Michael Zander, who was himself a member of the Royal Commission.

Lastly, the editors would like to thank the British Psychological Society for their support in organising the conference, and Mrs Arija Crux for her cheerful and valuable assistance producing this book.

David Morgan
Geoffrey M. Stephenson
June 1994

Contributors

John Baldwin is Professor of Judicial Administration at the University of Birmingham where he has been Director of the Institute of Judicial Administration since 1982. The three studies that he conducted under the auspices of the Royal Commission on Criminal Justice were published together in his report, *The Conduct of Police Investigations*.

Roger Evans is Professor of Socio-Legal Studies and Director of the School of Law, Social Work and Social Policy at Liverpool John Moores University. He has published widely on cautioning policy and practice and is author of the Royal Commission on Criminal Justice Research Report No. 8 on the conduct of police interviews with juveniles.

Gisli Gudjonsson is a Reader in Forensic Psychology at the Institute of Psychiatry, University of London, and is Head of the Adult National Clinical Psychology Services at the Maudsley and Bethlem Royal Hospitals. He was co-author of two reports for the Royal Commission on Criminal Justice and is the author of *The Psychology of Interrogations, Confessions and Testimony* (Wiley, 1992).

Roger Leng is a Senior Lecturer in Law at the University of Birmingham. He is co-author (with Colin Manchester) of *A Guide to the Criminal Justice Act 1991* (Fourmat) and (with Mike McConville and Andrew Sanders) *The Case for the Prosecution* (Routledge). His Royal Commission study, *The Right to Silence in Police Interrogation*, was published in 1993. In October 1994 he takes up a Readership in Law at the University of Warwick.

Mike Maguire Is Senior Lecturer in Criminology and Criminal Justice at the University of Wales, Cardiff. He has recently edited (with R. Reiner and R. Morgan) *The Oxford Handbook of Criminology* (Oxford University Press, 1994), and co-authored with C. Norris a report for the Royal Commission on

Criminal Justice (*The Conduct and Supervision of Criminal Investigations*, 1992).

David Morgan is Director of the Institute for Social Research and Senior Lecturer in Sociology at the University of Kent. His recent publications include (with Mary Evans) *The Battle for Britain: Citizenship and Ideology in the Second World War* (Routledge, 1993) and papers on civil society and social rights.

Stephen Moston is now a Lecturer in Psychology at the University of New South Wales, Australia. He is co-author (with Geoffrey Stephenson) of Royal Commission Report No. 22, *The Questioning and Interviewing of Suspects outside the Police Station*, and author of many articles on police interrogation and the right to silence.

Geoffrey M. Stephenson is Professor of Social Psychology at the University of Kent. He is author of *The Psychology of Criminal Justice* (Blackwell, 1993) and co-authored (with Stephen Moston) Research Report No. 22 for the Royal Commission, on police interviewing outside the station, and articles on police interrogation and the right to silence.

Tom Williamson is a Detective Chief Superintendent in the Metropolitan Police Service. A psychology graduate of the University of York, his research into strategic changes in police questioning led to the award of his doctorate from the University of Kent. He has conducted extensive research into the use of the right to silence.

Michael Zander is Professor of Law at the London School of Economics. He was a member of the Royal Commission on Criminal Justice and also chief author of the Royal Commission's *Crown Court Study* (Research Study No. 19, 1993). He is the author of numerous books and articles and was *The Guardian's* legal correspondent from 1963 to 1988.

Adrian Zuckerman is Fellow of University College, Oxford. He is author of *The Principles of Criminal Evidence* (Oxford University Press, 1989) and numerous articles on criminal and civil procedure.

Introduction: the Right to Silence in Criminal Investigations

David Morgan and Geoffrey M. Stephenson

This book addresses the controversial problems generated by the conflict between the duty of the police to interrogate those who they suspect have committed a criminal offence, and the right of citizens not to say anything that might be damaging to their interests. The whole issue is increasingly formulated in terms of simplistic dichotomies: do we favour the criminal's interests or society's? Should we retain a corrupt adversarial procedure or should we systematically seek the truth? Are we for individual liberty or the protection of society? We hope that readers of this book will come to appreciate the value of examining in some detail what is actually happening to suspects in police custody up and down the country before coming down one way or the other on an issue, the right to silence, that is presently dominating discussion of the Criminal Justice and Public Order Bill in Parliament.

Context of the debate

Until recently, the citizen's right to silence has seemed to be more secure than the police officer's obligation to interrogate. The unchallenged right of the police to question those they suspect of having committed a criminal offence is of relatively recent origin. It was formally acknowledged only in 1912, when the King's Bench judges, at the request of the Home Secretary, drew up the 'Judges' Rules', which briefly set out guidelines which the police were advised to follow when questioning suspects. Before that time, police could not rely on evidence derived from questioning necessarily being accepted in court (Williamson 1994). Only in 1978 were the Judges' Rules formally adopted by the Home Office, and a revised version published and circulated for the guidance of police officers in Home Office Circular 89/1978.

By way of contrast, the citizen's right to remain silent when accused of an offence has a long and respected history. As a privilege against self-incrimination the right to silence finds its origins in 17th-century revulsion against the interrogatory techniques of the Star Chamber of King Charles I (Easton 1991). In the United States, the right is embodied in the Constitution and is not challenged as it is now in Britain. As Easton (1991) points out, so great was the distrust of overbearing interrogations, and so great the wish to preserve the suspect from self-incrimination, that it was not until the passing of the Criminal Evidence Act 1898 that the accused became a competent witness in his or her own defence; but not, however, a compellable witness. The more recent Criminal Justice Act 1982 again clarifies the citizen's right to choose whether to testify on oath or to remain silent. That remains the position as Parliament now considers the provisions of a new Criminal Justice and Public Order Bill which proposes for the first time to limit in England the ancient privilege against self-incrimination.

From the time of its organisation by Sir Robert Peel in 1829, the police force gradually took over responsibility from the justices of the peace for pre-trial enquiry and the prosecution of offenders. The right to silence in response to police questioning was unquestioned, and accepted as a matter of course as being consistent with the ancient privilege against self-incrimination. Nowadays, the Codes of Practice issued under the Police and Criminal Evidence Act 1984, which currently govern police conduct, require 'the caution' to be administered before any period of questioning, the prescribed explanation of the caution specifying that it is given 'in pursuance of the general principle of English law that a person need not answer any questions or provide any information which might tend to incriminate him, and that no adverse inferences from this silence may be drawn at any trial that takes place' (Code of Practice C, note 10D).

In recent years the two issues of silence pre-trial and silence at trial have become separated, not least perhaps because the issue of police misconduct has relentlessly attracted public attention for three or more decades. Accusations of police corruption were headline news in the late 1960s, and they led in the Metropolitan Police to the dismissal and gaoling of a number of detective officers, the retirement of many more, and to the restructuring of the Criminal Investigation Department. More recently, a series of successful appeals against conviction, in which terrorist cases have featured strongly, has highlighted the extent to which police techniques of interrogation elicited false confessions and, more alarmingly, the extent to which police deliberately forged confessions. The fact that many of these miscarriages of justice took place before the Police and Criminal Evidence Act 1984 (PACE) was passed has done little to modify the dramatic impact of these cases. This has no doubt contributed to the fact that the recommendation of the Criminal Law Revision Committee (CLRC) in 1972 to modify the right to silence to permit juries to draw adverse inferences from a suspect's refusal to answer police questions has until recently found little favour amongst lawyers.

Besides the problem of controlling police enthusiasm for extracting confessions from reluctant and, sometimes, innocent suspects, recognition that we have an adversarial system of justice is fundamental to the argument in favour of retaining the right to silence. The recent Royal Commission on Criminal Justice in their report (1993) briefly but robustly defended our adversarial system against suggestions that (Continental) inquisitorial systems might provide justice more regularly. In addition to the 'fear of the consequences of an unsuccessful cultural transplant' (p. 4), the report argued that 'the roles of police, prosecutors and judges are as far as possible best kept separate and the judge who is responsible for the conduct of the trial is the arbiter of law but not of fact' (p. 4). Given this commitment to the adversarial principle it is not surprising that the Royal Commission decided not to support moves to modify or abolish the right to silence. They apparently accepted the logic of the argument that in an adversarial system of justice it is unwise if not improper to enact legislation which would materially detract from the prosecution's burden of proof.

We may well ask what in the present climate of opinion encourages and enables the government to press ahead with legislation to diminish the right to silence. There are two politically important issues, which we shall mention but briefly. First the seemingly inexorable growth of the crime rate lends persuasive power to the views of those, like the current Home Secretary, who believe that protecting the public from police misconduct is at odds with protecting the public from 'the criminal'. In his own words to the Conservative Party Conference:

In the last 30 years the balance in the criminal justice system has been tilted too far in favour of the criminal and against the protection of the public. The time has come to put that right. (Howard 1993.)

Secondly, one part of the United Kingdom – Northern Ireland – already is subject to the recommendations made by the CLRC for modification of the right to silence. Failure of a suspect to account to a police officer for presence in an area, or for articles, substances or marks on the person, may be commented on by the court, and may enter into the jury's evaluation of guilt. In addition, and in an attempt to nullify 'ambush' defences in court, the disclosure in court for the first time of previously undisclosed facts which were available to the suspect at the time of arrest may be adversely commented upon at trial. These, and additional restrictions on the right to silence in court were implemented swiftly and with little publicity, but have not been accomplished without criticism of the advantages taken by judges of their freedom to comment adversely on silence (Jackson 1991).

Most pertinently for our present discussion, however, is the fact that the provisions of PACE for the regulation of police interviews are being taken increasingly seriously by the police and, most importantly, by the judges. In other words, it can be argued that the effectiveness of PACE in keeping police conduct within acceptable limits demands that the right to silence be modified. Otherwise, the process of prosecution will be severely and unduly hampered.

PACE represented a major departure in the regulation of police conduct. Albeit with many qualifications, PACE ensured that, amongst other things, the rights of the suspect to legal representation, notification of relatives, and special protection in the case of minors and other vulnerable groups of persons, were now to be set out in codes of practice. In addition, codes of practice were drawn up to regulate the conduct of interviews by police officers, including provision for the introduction of audio tape recording of all interviews conducted at police stations. Moreover, all significant events whilst in custody would be monitored and recorded by a responsible custody sergeant. PACE did not change the law on the right to silence, despite the recommendations of the CLRC. However, police representatives argued then, as they do now, that as the provisions of PACE effectively dealt with the problem of the accuracy or content of confessions, it was now inappropriate to permit the criminal to enjoy the right to silence unhindered by judicial or prosecution comment of any kind.

The strength of this argument by the police depends, however, on evidence that the manner in which confessions were obtained was generally unexceptionable. In the words of the Act, a confession obtained by 'oppression' or 'in consequence of anything said or done which was likely, in the circumstances existing at the time, to render unreliable any confession which might be made' should not be allowed in evidence (PACE, s. 76(2)). Psychologists suggested in their evidence at the time (Irving and Hilgendorf 1980) that the very fact of arrest and detention is sufficiently 'oppressive' to call into question the reliability of many confessions obtained in such circumstances. That, it may be suggested, makes it all the more important for the police to behave with propriety towards detained suspects, and to avoid further increasing the sense of threat perceived by suspects.

The Act did not define oppression in precise terms, although it made clear that the onus was on the prosecution to demonstrate that an admission or damaging statement had been made in appropriate circumstances. It may be said that the Act, in its vagueness, was effectively inviting the judges themselves to define what was likely to render a confession unreliable

(Williamson 1994). In the event, case law has been slow to define the circumstances in which confessions may be deemed unreliable, but Williamson points to two recent cases which have clarified the issues somewhat. In the case of the 'Cardiff Three' (*R* v *Paris* (1992) 97 Cr App R 99) the Lord Chief Justice emphasised, in accordance with s. 76 of the Act, that the admissibility of a confession depends not on its truth but on the way it was obtained. Even more pertinently, Mr Justice Mitchell in *R* v *Heron*, excluded a confession of murder by the accused, 'regardless of the fact that his eventual confession may very well have been true'. This was because repetitive questioning of the accused, designed to 'break the defendant's resolve to make no admissions', had prevented the prosecution proving, as they were obliged to do, that the confession was not unreliable. The jury subsequently acquitted Mr Heron. Facing this robust interpretation of the requirements under PACE, the police will no doubt be confirmed in their view that the right to silence is an anachronism they can well do without.

The Royal Commission's advice to retain the right to silence and the existing caution, reflected to some extent their (majority) view that there was more to fear from the increased likelihood of false confessions by vulnerable persons, than there was to gain from any increased likelihood of conviction of the experienced and guilty criminal accustomed to sheltering behind the protection afforded by the right to silence. Their advice is also, as suggested earlier, consistent with their decision not to suggest modifications to our adversarial system of justice.

The Commission may have underestimated processes of change towards a less adversarial approach within the justice system, not least in the attitude of the police themselves. Following the establishment of the Crown Prosecution Service (CPS) in 1985 the police have naturally been less strongly identified with the process of prosecution, and there has in our view been an evident change in the attitudes and demeanour of the police at stages in the prosecution of alleged offenders. In particular, establishing the CPS, together with the necessity of painfully accommodating to the demands of PACE, has had the effect of strengthening the attractions to the police of their inquisitorial function. At its worst, this is seen in a 'take it or leave it' approach to the presentation of evidence to the CPS and to the courts. At its best, it is evident in profound changes in police perceptions of their investigative role (see chapter 7). If current training proves effective, then no longer will the police remorselessly seek confessions; rather they will 'interview for evidence', seeing themselves primarily as inquisitorial truth-seekers, albeit serving the needs of a (subsequently) adversarial contest in court. In court itself, the police already seem to respond with less alacrity to attempts by defence counsel to denigrate their evidence. The responsibility for outcomes is no longer theirs, and they can appear more as experts, less like combatants. There is perhaps a danger in the 'hands off' approach of the Royal Commission to the adversarial system, that other protagonists will not adjust sufficiently swiftly, or by themselves, to the new circumstances.

In bringing together the speakers at the conference, and again for this book, we made the assumption that the debate on the right to silence raised many questions of fact concerning police interviewing, its character and effects. A number of these had been addressed by academic researchers conducting work for the Royal Commission, and the conference was the first occasion they had for coming together to discuss the implications of their results.

The commissioned work which is discussed in this book, was conducted against the background of academic interest in the subject of police interviewing extending back a decade or two, and much relevant information was available before the Commission sat. Detailed studies of the behaviour of suspects in response to questioning, and the consequences for the process of prosecution, enable us to assess the validity of assumptions made by protagonists on both sides of the debate on the right to silence. An example comes from a study conducted in 1990 (Moston et al. 1993) which showed that police officers did, indeed, respond negatively to the exercise of silence by suspects whom they had interviewed. The effect of this, however, was to increase the likelihood that those maintaining silence would have charges preferred against them, at least when the evidence against the suspect was neither weak nor strong, but intermediate. Moreover, the exercise of silence did not affect the behaviour of the CPS; and subsequently at trial those who had maintained silence were more likely to be found guilty than those who had answered all questions. Maybe the police overestimate the difficulties caused by suspects who exercise their right not to answer questions. On the other hand, the same study indicated that, independently of other factors inducing suspects to confess, suspects are much more likely to remain silent when they have taken the advice of a solicitor. Police fears that uncooperative suspects are becoming a growing problem for them may well be correct, given the increasing prevalence of legal advice, frequently provided routinely and perfunctorily by unqualified representatives. However, as the following chapters indicate, abolition of the right to silence raises issues which go well beyond the immediate problem of redressing the balance between uncooperative suspects and the police.

The dispute over the right to silence

In the first chapter here, Roger Leng examines the debate surrounding these issues in the light of current research. The case for improving the procedures and efficiency of criminal investigations is not in dispute, but there are both principled and empirical objections to the Home Secretary's chosen means. The right that individuals should not be required to incriminate themselves traditionally safeguarded citizens from coercive and arbitrary powers of the State. Throughout the whole of the modern period, this common law tradition has been integral to an adversarial system of justice which places the onus of proof upon the prosecution, without assistance from the accused. The proposals before Parliament in the government's Criminal Justice and Public Order Bill alter this right in ways which critics claim threaten the integrity of a fundamental principle which has upheld the autonomy and privacy of citizens for more than two hundred years (Easton 1991). In short, opponents of the Bill argue that the right to silence is a basic right of constitutional significance and should not be unceremoniously abolished for wholly utilitarian or political gains.

Reviewing the legal implications of the present Bill, Leng points out that clauses 29 and 30 permit adverse inferences to be drawn if someone fails to account for his or her behaviour, or objects and substances in his or her possession, or for his or her presence near the scene of a crime. Similar inferences could be drawn in court if a defendant had previously refused to answer questions raised by the police. There is concern amongst lawyers and civil liberties groups that these provisions — which have operated in Northern Ireland since 1988 — will increase the pressures on suspects questioned by the police and, especially in the case of vulnerable persons, lead to more false confessions and miscarriages of justice. These concerns were considered by the Royal Commission on Criminal Justice which recommended that the right to silence should be retained.

The main objection to the proposed changes is that silence may be interpreted as an indication of guilt and used in evidence against the accused. Against this, the Home Secretary has emphasised that individuals have a duty to cooperate with the police. In practice, it is claimed, the only real reason for refusing to answer questions is to evade an admission of guilt. In this respect, the right to silence protects criminals by obstructing the police in their enquiries and withholds material evidence from the courts.

The substantive issues in the debate are therefore whether silence is an indication of guilt; whether altering the right to silence would place innocent suspects at greater risk of wrongful conviction, or whether, as the police and the Home Secretary believe, it would lead to the proper conviction of more guilty offenders. In a persuasive critique, Leng examines the research evidence on each of these questions and the often simplistic interpretations which have informed the present debate. However, the underlying issue, he suggests, is not how often or in what circumstances the right to silence is exercised, but the significance which critics and advocates of abolition attach to suspects' rights.

7

Opinion on this matter has recently been sharpened by a succession of dramatic miscarriages of justice which undermined public confidence in the police and raised serious concerns about the conduct of police investigations. To a certain extent, these cases (notably, the Guildford Four, the Maguires, the Birmingham Six) have shifted the terms of the debate by focussing attention upon whether existing safeguards provide adequate protection against unfair and oppressive methods of interrogation and the abuse of suspects detained by the police. These manifest concerns led to the Royal Commission on Criminal Justice and informed its recommendations on measures to improve the reliability and quality of police evidence.

It could be argued, however, that concern over these much publicised cases is largely misplaced. The cases in question pre-date the Police and Criminal Evidence Act 1984 and the related Codes of Practice which recognise stricter and more comprehensive safeguards against police malpractice (Home Office, 1985; 1991). There is now a legal requirement that interviews with suspects should be recorded on tape and, if required, reproduced in court. Furthermore, suspects have the right to a legal advisor during police interrogations and, in the case of juveniles and other conspicuously vulnerable persons, an 'appropriate adult' should be present during interviews. These and other provisions, give rise to what Greer (1990) refers to as the 'exchange-abolitionist' argument. This claims that with the introduction of PACE and the new Codes of Practice, the traditional right to silence has been superseded by considerably enhanced safeguards and thus may be safely removed.

Evidence on police methods and procedures

The next five papers in this collection test the strength and reliability of this claim. The authors draw upon research, including their own studies for the Royal Commission, specifically designed to assess the practical implications of these new provisions in the period post-PACE. In the order discussed here, they examine: (a) the supervision of criminal investigations; (b) the preliminary questioning of suspects; (c) the conduct of police interrogations and the role of legal advisers; (d) the treatment of juvenile suspects, and (e) the identification of psychologically vulnerable persons detained for questioning. In each case, research is based upon close examination of the procedures and working assumptions observed in routine criminal investigations. The accumulated evidence offers an authoritative account of the transactions between suspects and the police, and a firm empirical basis on which to judge the Home Secretary's assurances that the right to silence is an anachronistic impediment we could well do without.

Support for these assurances comes mainly from the police themselves. Their submission to the Royal Commission (Police Service 1991) claims that under the new guidelines criminal investigations are closely supervised by responsible officers and interviews are now less concerned with extracting confessions than establishing the truth. In chapter 2, Maguire argues that some advances have been made in these directions in the last few years — due partly to the influence of the Royal Commission itself — but evidence from contemporary research suggests that supervision and accountability in criminal investigations are still relatively lax. Maguire found that suspects are still commonly arrested on little or no evidence; custody officers exercise minimum control, while interrogations typically press for confessions rather than critically search for the truth. It should be emphasised that there is no suggestion here of police malpractice or collusion: Maguire's point is that, with a few exceptions (such as regional crime squads and special units), the organisation and culture of a typical criminal investigation department is not geared to routine, methodical investigations, either before or after an arrest. For the most part, CID work is unpredictable, heavily bureaucratic and under-resourced. Officers are under continual pressures from mounting case loads, administrative changes and senior colleagues, as well as from politicians and the media to produce better results. In response to this 'chaotic' environment, Maguire found that police tactics tend to be reactive and highly individualistic, relying on the largely unsupervised initiatives of relatively junior officers to get results. The situation is far removed from the strategically planned and rationally coordinated model of crime management and prevention recommen-ded by the Audit Commission's recent report (1993). Inevitably, it is open to 'rule-bending' and tactical abuses which, as Maguire says, go mostly unheeded and seldom formally disciplined by senior staff.

Moston and Stephenson (chapter 3) draw attention to the fact that what happens at the police station is only part of the process of investigating an offence. Many suspects are questioned prior to arrest, mostly at the scene of the crime or at home. Unlike interviews which have to be tape-recorded, 'questioning' a suspect or witness is regarded as a distinct activity and is not subject to the same controls (Code C: 'Notes for Guidance', 11A, p. 60). There is growing concern, however, that under the pretext of 'ordinary' questioning, officers may take advantage of relatively unsupervised situations to use improper or persuasive tactics which could influence the outcome of a subsequent recorded interview. Indeed, Moston and Stephenson found that suspects interviewed in relatively informal settings showed a marked tendency to admit offences. Very few of these interviews were recorded, either in writing or on tape, at the time they took place. The study concludes that, for whatever reason, suspects are more vulnerable to incriminating admissions when interviewed outside a police station. One implication of these findings is that formally recorded interviews cannot be taken as a complete or reliable account of transactions between a suspect and the police. What happens between police officers and suspects preceding these interviews appears to affect the outcome of the interview itself, and hence raises doubts about the spontaneity and integrity of evidence presented on tape.

Questions about the reliability of evidence obtained in interviews and, more generally, the conduct of police interrogations, proved decisive in the miscarriages of justice which led to the Royal Commission and figured prominently on its research agenda. After considering submissions on the present state of police interviewing, the Royal Commission took the view that whilst PACE and existing Codes of Practice were generally progressive and fair, additional safeguards were necessary to protect suspects from 'oppressive tactics', especially in the case of juvenile and vulnerable suspects who are at risk of making false confessions. However, Baldwin argues in chapter 4 that the Commission missed a significant opportunity to tighten present guidelines by clarifying the limits of acceptable interrogation and particularly the nature of 'oppression' which at present has no precise meaning in law. The Commission's reticence on these questions is also picked up in the following chapter by Evans who criticises the Commission's failure to address these fundamental points and recommend appropriate legal reforms. What is at issue here is the extent to which a suspect may be coerced, manipulated or otherwise induced to be an unwitting agent of their own conviction. In practice, this has as much to do with the organisation and 'culture' of the police as the rights of suspects in law.

Both aspects of the problem are raised by Baldwin in discussing the role of legal advisers in formal interviews. He begins by reminding us that the quality of police interviewing is highly variable and rarely resembles the sharply scripted exchanges portrayed on television. Interviewers are frequently nervous, aggressive and surprisingly inept. From the outset, officers tend to presume a suspect's guilt, whether there is strong corroborative evidence or not, and not uncommonly resort to harrying tactics or unfair inducements to secure a confession. Of the 600 recorded interviews Baldwin examined, one in three fell short of reasonable standards of good practice (Baldwin 1992).

The generally unimpressive standard of interviewing may well reflect a lack of training in more sophisticated and ethical techniques — a point strongly endorsed by Williamson in chapter 7. Yet Baldwin doubts whether more effective training is enough: the problem he suggests is 'deep-rooted and endemic' in the culture and resistance of the police to change. This places legal advisers, who are often junior and relatively inexperienced, in an invidious position both in relation to their clients and the police. Confronted by an environment which is suspicious, if not openly dismissive of legal representations, there is a tendency for legal advisers to adopt an acquiescent and conciliatory stance, rather than place their client's and their own interests at risk. These difficulties are further exacerbated by the uncertainties and ambiguities surrounding the legal adviser's role. Baldwin points out, for instance, that it is not known whether the police are at liberty to ignore objections from legal representatives over such crucial matters as the conduct of interviews. It is difficult to see how the abolition of the right to silence could fail to shift this already unequal balance of power even further in favour of the police.

These outstanding difficulties between the legal profession and police were recognised by the Royal Commission. However, there was little attempt to redress the balance by clarifying apparent inconsistencies in the Code of Practice which defines the role of legal advisers in relation to the police. As things now stand, Baldwin concludes that the legal and procedural rules relating to the role of legal advisers and the conduct of interviews remain confusing and ineffectually vague.

It should be remembered that a significant proportion of suspects questioned by the police are juveniles. Concern that young persons may be especially vulnerable to manipulative or coercive methods of interrogation is recognised under PACE which allows for an 'appropriate adult' to be present whenever a juvenile is interviewed in connection with a criminal offence. There is a clear expectation that the accompanying adult should advise the suspect, facilitate communication, and ensure that the interview is conducted properly and fairly (Code C, para. 11.16). Despite these safeguards, there is cause for continuing concern. Drawing upon his research for the Royal Commission, Evans reports (chapter 5) that in the vast majority of cases, the adult in question (usually a parent or social worker) made no contribution at all to the proceedings, whilst the few who intervened were as likely to collude with the police as support the accused. In general, juvenile suspects appear to be poorly served and poorly informed of their rights. Evans found that juveniles are routinely arrested on a presumption of guilt, detained, sometimes for lengthy periods in police cells, while their distress and inexperience is commonly exploited in interviews. However, juveniles rarely exercise the right to silence, even though nearly 40 per cent of the suspects in Evans's sample were not told why they were being held at any stage during the formal interview. The situation did not appear to improve when a legal representative was present. Furthermore, suspects were liable to be cautioned even though they had failed to make a clear confession or had denied involvement in an offence. The use of a caution in such cases, Evans suggests, amounts to a substantial miscarriage of justice, against which there is no redress.

The risks, not least of false confession, amongst young persons are evident. However, there are other categories of person whose evidence may be similarly at risk. Provisions are made under PACE for suspects with special difficulties, such as deafness, mental handicap, mental illness, or temporarily disturbed mental states who may not fully understand the questions put to them and whose evidence may not be reliable. In such cases, the police are responsible for identifying vulnerable suspects and, as in the case of juveniles, calling an 'appropriate adult'. However, in the last of the empirical studies reported here, Gudjonsson draws our attention to other less conspicuous conditions which may affect a suspect's behaviour and the reliability of his or her evidence under stress. The susceptibility of some suspects to give in to leading questions, or their tendency to comply or acquiesce under pressure, or to incriminate themselves by filling gaps in their memory with imagined events, are not likely to be obvious to police officers seeking a confession. These tendencies have been carefully documented by Gudjonsson elsewhere (Gudjonsson 1992). Here, he presents a profile of the psychological characteristics of a cross-section of ordinary adult suspects, and observes the extent to which the police identified vulnerable persons at risk.

It is apparent from this study that the police routinely deal with persons of less than average intelligence and ability, many of whom may have difficulties understanding their legal rights. In some cases, suspects were unable to make competent sense of the standard 'Notice to Detained Persons' which includes a caution and a summary of detainees' rights. Gudjonsson found that the average reading age amongst the 173 suspects examined was under 12 years. Seventy per cent of these suspects were unemployed. It might be thought that these characteristics would render most suspects sufficiently vulnerable to manipulative or persuasive interrogation to warrant the presence of a competent adviser: on stricter criteria, Gudjonsson found 'good clinical reasons' in 25 cases to call an appropriate adult. Most of these suspects showed conspicuous signs of mental illness, mental handicap or abnormal psychological states. In the event, the police called an appropriate adult in less than a third of these cases.

The study concludes that police officers should be given basic training in identifying vulnerable suspects to ensure that legal rights are protected and the evidence obtained in interviews is reliable, admissible and fair. This recommendation was adopted by the Royal Commission, yet it raises again the more general question of whether training alone is sufficient to effect necessary changes in the methods and expectations of the police. We return to this question in the next two chapters which discuss the possible direction and obstacles to change.

The case for change

The Police and Criminal Evidence Act made significant changes to the legal framework and procedures relating to criminal investigations. These developments have been cited as grounds for altering the right to silence, not least by the police. However, we should be careful not to confuse administrative changes with everyday practices and routines. The research evidence considered here suggests there are few grounds for supposing risks of malpractice have been substantially reduced. All too often, suspects are liable to be arrested on little or no evidence and subjected to improper or oppressive questioning, even though interviews are formally recorded and often take place in the presence of legal advisers or others. On balance, despite the introduction of PACE, progress appears to have been of modest dimensions.

The Royal Commission's Report made a number of specific recommendations intended to curb some of the more hazardous practices placing suspects at risk. Yet Baldwin and Evans argue that these only obliquely address fundamental problems inherent in the construction and reliability of police evidence. Some of these concerns became evident in the case of George Heron, mentioned above. The case amply demonstrates that the vulnerability of suspects depends not only upon their psychological state, but the methods of interrogation employed by the police. Although the right to silence may protect a person from incriminating themselves (or others), it does not prevent the police from asking questions, over and over again. The point at which the cumulative effect of relentless, repetitive questioning becomes 'oppressive' and places the suspect's testimony at risk, has now been recognised by Mr Justice Mitchell who reviewed the Heron tapes. As this case showed, the right to silence is a poor defence against determined and concerted efforts to extract a confession in the face of repeated denials. More generally, it raises questions about the assumptions which underlie the production of criminal evidence and the relationship of the police to the prosecution case. These questions are taken up in the chapters by Williamson and Zuckerman below.

Zuckerman identifies bias and suggestibility as virtually insuperable obstacles in the search for truth. Police interviews tend to begin on a presumption of guilt and proceed in search of confirming evidence while ignoring awkward anomalies and denials. There are serious risks that constructive bias may harden speculative suspicions into objective, but unconfessed truths. The fact that a good many suspects are eventually persuaded to confess, re-enforces the belief that most suspects are culpable and encourages the police to see themselves as expert arbiters of truth. In this context, we should also remember that the police are continually under pressure to perform with better results. Persuading a suspect to confess is a cheap, readily available and relatively effective method of resolving crimes. There is seldom time or the resources to 'follow up and check' a suspect's account, as the Royal Commission suggests. Indeed, as resources decline in relation to the prevalence of reported crime, persuasive methods of interrogation are an economical response to pressures for better clear-up rates: as we know, there is a predictable association between confessions and expectations of conviction (McConville, et al. 1991), and convictions are a telling indicator of effective performance and the efficiency of the police.

Given the conflicting demands upon the police and the related tendencies towards bias, the question is whether interrogations can be both effective *and* ethically accountable? The problem is addressed by Williamson in chapter 7. He argues that recent miscarriages of justice have forced a 'fundamental reappraisal' of the role of the police in an adversarial system of justice. Aggressive and manipulative methods of interrogation and an over-reliance on confessions are symptoms, he suggests, of the close link between the investigative role of the police and the prosecution and conviction of the accused. However, the risks of malpractice would diminish, he suggests, if the inquisitorial functions of the police were separate and autonomous from the adversarial process in court. The police could then redefine their role as impartial and expert investigators who establish the facts while leaving their interpretation and legal implications to the courts.

The argument is consistent with the principles of a new approach to investigative interviewing, which Williamson has done much to promote. This new approach emphasises the need for a more objective and critical stance in assessing evidence; the fair and courteous treatment of all suspects, and special consideration for vulnerable suspects at risk. Contrary to the dissenting view that PACE has already effectively de-skilled experienced investigators by imposing inhibiting codes and constraints (a sentiment echoed by more than a few police officers attending the conference at Kent), Williamson defends these new principles and the associated training programme on the pragmatic grounds that they have been shown to be more effective than the traditionally more 'robust' approach. Moreover, Williamson argues that responsible and effective questioning eliminates the need for a right to silence. He believes that judges would be very unlikely to admit confession evidence, or anything else, that was not consistent with the standards and principles of 'investigative interviewing'.

The strength of this approach lies in the relative autonomy of investigators from the prosecution which favours a more detached and critical appraisal of evidence and promises to raise the general level of scepticism amongst the police. However, this brings us back to Zuckerman's analysis of the 'cognitive obstacles' to accurate and reliable investigative work. In this instance, Zuckerman's critique is directed more specifically at the Royal Commission's Report than the assumptions and practices of the police. He suggests that the Commission's recommendations to counter distortion and bias appear to be informed by the innocent belief that 'evidence' consists of raw, unmediated facts. Zuckerman suggests the alternative view that criminal evidence is the outcome of an interactive process in which the police construct an account of reality which fits their presuppositions and beliefs. As he says, this is not 'an accurate, disinterested snapshot of past events': it is the production of an unequal process of negotiation in which fact, speculation and inference all play a part. Yet this is the account on which the accused will be tried. The idea that we will get closer to the truth by modifying the rules of interviewing, or the use of tape recorders, or by encouraging training, is wholly illusory. Bias and suggestibility, he believes, call for more radical changes than technical adjustments, however sensible, to existing Home Office codes. Given that a trial is not an enquiry into what really happened, but an examination of the police investigation, would it not be sensible, he asks, for the suspect's solicitor to play a more critical role in the proceedings in order to counter speculative bias and distortion as the police case proceeds?

In defence of silence

The final chapter in this collection makes a spirited case against abolishing the right to silence. In a polemical argument, Michael Zander reviews the history of the debate since the Criminal Law Revision Committee proposed the abolition of the right to silence in 1972. The Committee's proposal sank in a sea of controversy: 20 years later, it has been salvaged by the Criminal Justice Bill. In the meantime, two Royal Commissions have carefully examined the issues and made principled recommendations that the right to silence should be retained. On both occasions, the Commission argued that alterations to the right of silence would place unfair pressures on suspects and increase the risk of wrongful convictions. In the absence of further evidence to the contrary, it has to be assumed that the Home Secretary has decided to ignore the Royal Commission's advice for expedient reasons alone.

Zander questions the constitutional propriety of this decision. Removing the right to silence raises matters of fundamental principle on which the Royal Commission was specifically asked to advise. Moreover, it is a principle on which it would be entirely appropriate for the views of a Royal Commission to hold sway. Zander believes that ignoring the advice of a Royal Commission on such an exceptional matter 'verges on the unconstitutional'.

However, his main objection brings us back to the central concerns of the preceding chapters. He argues there is already a substantial body of research and expert opinion which indicates that removing the right to silence will probably have little or no influence on whether suspects cooperate with the police. This is even more likely in the case of experienced criminals and terrorists who are believed to be exploiting the right. In other words, abolishing the right to silence is unlikely to have the effect the Home Secretary intends: indeed, as Zander explains, it could be counter-productive by making matters appreciably worse for the police.

The view is consistent with the experience of Northern Ireland where the right to silence was abolished for all offences in 1988. Since 1988, there has been no indication that suspects detained in Northern Ireland have been more willing to cooperate with the police, or are less likely to remain silent, than suspects in England and Wales. These observations are especially relevant as proposals to restrict the right to silence in the Criminal Justice Bill follow the same form as the Order applied in Northern Ireland (Jackson 1991; Justice 1994).

Why then should the government move to abolish the right to silence in defiance of two Royal Commissions and against the weight of expert opinion and advice? The belief that it will lead to the conviction of substantially more guilty offenders appears to be contrary to accumulated experience and research. At present, there appears to be no evidence that removing the right to silence will significantly alter the behaviour of suspects questioned by the police. Nor is it a likely deterrent to crime. However, the explanation may have less to do with the balance of evidence than the Home Secretary's response to the recent direction of progressive reforms.

Since the introduction of PACE, there has been a rational attempt to improve the efficiency of criminal investigations and the reliability of evidence presented in court. Much of this effort has been aimed at strengthening the professional and ethical accountability of the police. It has been supported on a broad front by two Royal Commissions, the Home Office, lawyers' associations, civil liberties groups and by far-sighted police officers. These developments have been accepted in principle within the police service itself. Williamson cites the *Statement of Common Purpose and Values* which enjoins officers to be professional, fair, helpful and reassuring, and 'to respond to well founded criticism with a willingness to change'. These sentiments underpin the principles of 'investigative interviewing' and suggest real progress has been made in an organisation which in the past has been fiercely resistant to change. The government's intention to abolish the right to silence sends a different message to the police. In particular, it undermines pains-taking efforts to encourage police officers to produce fair and credible evidence by sanctioning the belief that silence alone is evidence of guilt. This is likely to influence the conduct of both formal interviews and exchanges with suspects on the street. As Leng argues, these changes 'will amount to no less than a counter-revolution in police investigations' and end an era which promised progressive and continuing reforms on the basis of careful research. Indeed, it is difficult to avoid the inference that abolishing the right to silence signals the government's greater concern with the politics of law and order than the rational development of the criminal justice system and the value of critical research.

References

Audit Commission (1993), *Helping with Enquiries: Tackling Crime Effectively* (London: Audit Commission).

Baldwin, J. (1992), *Video Taping Police Interviews with Suspects: an Evaluation* (Police Research Series Paper 1) (London: Home Office, Police Research Group).

Criminal Law Revision Committee (1972) *Eleventh Report: Evidence (General)* (Cmnd 4991) (London: HMSO).

Easton, S. (1991), *The Right to Silence* (Aldershot: Avebury).

Greer, S. (1990), 'The right to silence: a review of the current debate', *Modern Law Review*, vol. 53, p. 709.

Gudjonsson, G.H. (1992), *The Psychology of Interrogations, Confessions and Testimony* (Chichester: Wiley).

Howard, Michael (1993), Home Secretary's speech to the Conservative Party annual conference, Blackpool, 6 October 1993 (London: Home Office).

Irving B., and Hilgendorf, L. (1980) *Police Interrogation: the Psychological Approach* (Royal Commission on Criminal Procedure Research Study No. 1) (London: HMSO).

Jackson, J.D. (1991), 'Curtailing the right to silence: lessons from Northern Ireland', *Criminal Law Review*, p. 404.

JUSTICE (1994), 'The Right of Silence Debate: The Northern Ireland Experience', May 1994.

McConville, M., Sanders, A., and Leng, R. (1991) *The Case for the Prosecution: Police Suspects and the Construction of Criminality* (London: Routledge).

Moston, S., Stephenson, G.M., and Williamson, T.M. (1993), 'The incidence, antecedents and consequences of the use of the right to silence during police questioning', *Criminal Behaviour and Mental Health*, vol. 3, pp. 30–47.

Police Service (1991), *Evidence from the Police Service in England and Wales to the Royal Commission on Criminal Justice*. Unpublished.

Royal Commission on Criminal Justice (1993), *Report* (Cm 2263) (London: HMSO).

Williamson, T.M. (1994), 'Interviewing for evidence: developing a legal framework'. Unpublished manuscript.

1

The Right-to-Silence Debate

Roger Leng

The right to silence has traditionally operated in two contexts: the investigation and the trial. In both contexts, the right has similar roots, notably the twin principles that a citizen should not be required to incriminate him or herself and that the burden of proving guilt should rest upon the prosecution. In either context the issue whether the right should be retained or abolished is subject to similar considerations. Indeed, the package of measures contained in the Criminal Justice and Public Order Bill[1] published in December 1993 would abrogate the right in both contexts. However, although this linkage is acknowledged, the purpose of the present paper is to review the current debate about silence during the investigation and to consider what light modern research can shed on some of the issues at the core of that debate.

The right to silence in police interrogation

The right to silence in relation to criminal investigations is expressed through a number of separate rules governing the relationship between the police and the citizen, and the conduct of the trial. Thus, it has been held that, short of the power of arrest, a citizen cannot be required to remain at a particular place to answer police questions and that refusal to answer police questions cannot amount to the offence of obstruction of a constable (*Rice* v *Connolly* [1966] 2 QB 414). At trial, the judge is barred from suggesting to the jury that inferences might be drawn against a defendant merely because he or she had declined to answer some or all questions during police interview (Easton 1991, pp. 9–16).

---

[1] All references to clauses in the Bill are numbered as in its first published version (House of Commons Bill 9 Session 1993/94).

It is also good practice for trial judges to remind juries that a defendant who declined to answer some police questions was perfectly entitled to do so.

The right to silence is also reflected in procedural rules regulating the treatment of suspects. Thus a suspect must be cautioned on arrest and prior to interview that he or she is not required to say anything, but that anything said may be given in evidence (PACE Code C, sect. 10). The right to silence is also indirectly protected by the suspect's right to consult a solicitor in the police station (PACE, s. 58) and to have a legal adviser present during any police interview.

However, although silence does not attract a formal sanction, in practice the right is substantially curtailed by the indirect adverse consequences which may flow from exercising it. Thus, there is nothing to stop the police from continuing to question, and PACE legitimates longer periods of detention for silent suspects on the basis that until the suspect speaks the need to detain for questioning remains (PACE, s. 37(2)).

The fact that the suspect remains silent in the police station may also prejudice any attempt to raise a defence in court. It has long been established that in such circumstances a judge can instruct a jury to bear in mind that the police have not had the opportunity to test the suspect's defence by investigation. Indeed, although the terms of judicial comment are strictly limited, in practice there is nothing to stop a jury or bench of magistrates equating silence with guilt. The scope for doing this is clearly indicated by the Crown Court study which found that where the suspect had remained silent, this fact become known to the jury in 79–85% of cases (Zander and Henderson 1993).

The popular conception of silence is that it is an easy low-risk route for the guilty to avoid conviction. This view ignores the reality of the criminal trial. Except where the police have no evidence at all, silence is clearly a high-risk option which should not be undertaken or advised easily.

The debate

Although deeply rooted in our legal traditions, the right to silence has always attracted serious criticisms. These criticisms have been persistently voiced by the police (Mark 1973; ACPO 1993), who see the right as hampering their efforts to prosecute criminals, and by some members of the judiciary (Lawton 1987; Lord Lane in *R* v *Alladyce* (1988) 87 Cr App R 380; Taylor 1994). These criticisms have been endorsed by the Criminal Law Revision Committee (1972) and the Home Office Working Group on the Right to Silence (1989) who successively recommended the abolition of the right.

The major grounds of criticism can be simply summarised:

(a) *Unprincipled.* It is argued that investigating crime and law enforcement are functions carried out for the benefit of the community as a whole, and that in principle citizens should be under a duty to cooperate and answer questions when required.

(b) *Pointless.* It is argued that there is no point in preserving the right if it serves only to aid criminals to evade justice.

(c) *Illogical.* It is argued that the only real reason for silence is guilt, and it is therefore illogical to bar judges from directing juries that guilt may be inferred from silence.

(d) *Perversion of justice.* It is argued that protection of the right to silence may pervert justice because it withholds cogent evidence from the jury.

(e) *Obstruction of investigations.* It is argued that investigations are hampered where suspects exercise the right to silence because the police are denied evidence from the best source — the suspect.

Similarly powerful counter-arguments that the right expresses a vital constitutional principle and provides an important safeguard for suspects, are expressed by civil libertarian groups (Thornton et al. 1992) and some lawyers' organisations (Law Society 1992; LAG 1991). These arguments have influenced both the Royal Commission on Criminal Procedure (1981) and the Royal Commission on Criminal Justice (1993) to recommend retention of the right. The arguments for retention can be simply summarised:

(a) *Privilege against self-incrimination.* It is argued that the common law tradition is that no citizen should be required by law to incriminate him or herself.

(b) *Burden of proof.* It is argued that no citizen should be punished until the State has demonstrated guilt beyond reasonable doubt. This principle would be undermined if the suspect's silence could be treated as evidence against him or her and thereby reduce the State's burden of proving guilt.

(c) *Usurpation of trial.* It is argued that the proper place to hear evidence and determine guilt or innocence is the trial, with all of the safeguards which attach thereto. To force the suspect to participate in a pre-trial interview for the purpose of determining the facts is to usurp the trial.

(d) *Risks in interview.* It is argued that in the coercive atmosphere of the police interview, vulnerable and suggestible suspects may be induced to incriminate themselves falsely. The ultimate safeguard against this is to remain silent.

As well as the broad issue of principle whether or not the right to silence should be retained or abolished, there is a second level of debate about how the right should be abolished.

Two major models for reform have emerged (Zander 1993b). The first model was introduced by the Criminal Law Revision Committee in 1972 and subsequently adopted and developed by the Home Office Working Group (HOWG) in 1989. Under the HOWG proposals, a suspect who had been silent at interview but subsequently raised a defence in court would be subject to cross-examination about the earlier failure to mention the defence. The judge and counsel for both sides would then be free to comment on the silence at interview, and to invite the jury to draw appropriate inferences.

In order to warn the suspect of the possible consequences of silence, HOWG recommended a new caution to be administered prior to arrest, interview and charge. Under the proposed caution the suspect would be warned that if he or she wished to rely upon a defence it would be best to mention it to the police and that failure to do so might lead to the defence being disbelieved.

The second and more radical model has operated in Northern Ireland since 1988 (Ruddell 1990; Jackson 1990; 1991; 1993) and forms the basis of the government's proposed reforms set out in the Criminal Justice and Public Order Bill. The Bill follows the HOWG scheme in permitting inferences to be drawn against a defendant who raises a defence at trial having been silent at interview. Although the bill makes no reference to pre-interview cautions it is certain that the PACE codes will be revised to require a new form of caution as recommended by HOWG. The Bill, however, goes considerably beyond the HOWG model by permitting inferences to be drawn from an accused person's failure to account for incriminating objects or substances in his or her possession or marks on his or her clothing, or from his or her failure to account for presence near the scene of a crime.

Both models of reform would amount to an abolition of the accused's right to silence, since under both schemes silence would be transformed from a neutral factor into positive evidence for the prosecution. The proposals in the 1994 Bill would attach considerable risks to silence since it could be treated as evidence against the accused whether or not he or she chose to raise a specific defence in court.

The scheme in the Bill would also apparently encourage officers to reverse current practice and ask significant questions at the scene of arrest. This will generate its own problems of proof. Tape recording has largely put an end to disputes about what was actually said during formal interview. If, however, inferences may be drawn from silence in the street, then once again the courts will be faced with the impossible task of deciding who is telling the truth where constable and suspect disagree about what was said on arrest.

The interrogation context

It is not uncommon for discussions about the right to silence to be conducted at the level of constitutional principle, whilst ignoring the practical context of

the investigation and prosecution of crime. But this is untenable. Probably the major objective for those who seek to abolish or modify the right to silence is to encourage more suspects to answer police questions (or perhaps to reverse the trend towards the 'no comment' interview). The police believe that this would lead to more confessions. Since we know that there is a strong correlation between confessions and convictions (McConville and Baldwin 1981, ch. 6), it is perhaps not unreasonable to assume that abolition would lead to more convictions.

Quite apart from the possibility of generating more confessions, changing the law as proposed in the 1994 Bill would lend a new significance to police interviews since they would be a potential source of evidence whether or not the suspect answered or was silent. This would further emphasise the primacy of the interview as the major technique of evidence collection and would tend to shift the determination of guilt or innocence from the court to the police station.

Whether or not such radical changes are appropriate or desirable can be decided only on the basis of a detailed consideration of the role of interrogation in the process of investigation. It would be necessary to consider the effectiveness of police interviews in generating evidence, and the quality of the evidence so produced. Particular attention should be paid to whether or not interview techniques are capable of eliciting a balanced account and to the question of the reliability of confessions. Similarly, the extent of informal off-the-record discussions and their impact on the formal interview would have to be considered (Moston and Stephenson, 1993; Leng 1994). Overarching these considerations is the question of the effectiveness of active safeguards, such as tape-recording and legal advice as well as of *ex post facto* safeguards such as the exclusion of evidence.

Research on silence — the numbers game

As discussed above the right to silence debate is not self-contained and necessarily feeds upon more general research into the investigation of crime. There is, however, a body of work dealing directly with the issue of silence. With three notable exceptions (Moston et al. 1993; McConville and Hodgson 1993; Leng 1993) this research has been concerned almost exclusively with estimating the extent of exercise of the right.

One unfortunate consequence of this continued emphasis on the numbers of silent suspects is that it encourages the simplistic argument that the larger the number relying on the right, the stronger the case for abolition. Another way of putting this argument is that the right to silence is fine as long as nobody actually exercises it. This view is implicit in the commentary to the recent ACPO study (1993).

22

An alternative approach is that the figures are a neutral factor in the debate: if the right is a good thing then high figures are correspondingly good; if the right is a bad thing then high figures indicate a problem. This approach refocuses the debate on the central question: whether or not the right to silence is a good thing. In turn this question can be broken down into three key issues: (a) whether as a matter of fact silence is indicative of guilt; (b) whether (as the civil libertarians argue) silence provides a necessary safeguard for the suspect; and (c) whether (as the police argue) abolition of the right would lead to the proper conviction of more guilty offenders.

However, although numbers should not dominate the debate, it remains important to address the question of numbers for two reasons: first, in order to calculate the potential effects of abolishing the right; secondly, because realistically it seems clear that numbers will retain a potent force in the continuing political debate.

There have been more than a dozen authoritative estimates of silence in interview (reviewed in Leng 1993, ch. 2) since Michael Zander pioneered empirical research on the issue with his Old Bailey study of 1979. Estimates have varied widely between 5 per cent and 23 per cent, although this variation probably reflects differences in sampling and methodology rather than divergences in practice. Thus, higher rates of silence are recorded in relation to samples of CID cases, and samples of interviews chosen for video recording, as opposed to samples of all cases in which interviews are held. Similarly, higher rates are found in relation to contested Crown Court cases as opposed to samples of all cases coming to court.

All studies prior to those carried out for the Royal Commission on Criminal Justice can be criticised on the basis that they treat the identification of cases involving exercise of the right to silence as unproblematic. None indicates the circumstances in which it is considered that the right to silence is exercised. Presumably, any suspect who declines to answer some questions at some stage of the interview, is treated as exercising the right.

This simplistic approach to definition may be challenged. The debate about silence is fundamentally a debate about whether silence amounts to a problem and whether the law should be reformed to deal with that problem. If calculations of the extent of silence are to inform the debate, it is arguable that the only cases which should be counted are those in which the perceived problem of silence arises and on which the proposed reform of the law would have an impact. Following this approach, two categories of case in which the suspect declines to answer some questions should not be counted as involving a significant exercise of the right to silence.

The first category relates to refusal to answer questions which are irrelevant to the investigation. Recent studies by Baldwin (1993) and by McConville and

Hodgson (1993) make clear that such questioning is common. Abolition of the right to silence would permit adverse inverences to be drawn from refusal to answer allegations. But there could be no question of drawing an evidential inference against a suspect who refused to answer an irrelevant question. Accordingly, refusal to answer such questions should not be counted as a significant exercise of the right to silence.

The second category consists of cases in which a suspect answers particular questions, having initially refused to do so. In these cases silence may have presented a problem for the investigators — but it is a problem which is dealt with in the course of the interview. Once all relevant questions have been answered there is no outstanding problem which needs to be dealt with by law reform.

There is also a further group of cases which *should* be considered as involving exercise of the right, which would be missed by simply counting refusals to answer. This group consists of cases in which the suspect answers all questions, but later in court raises a defence which he or she had not previously mentioned, having had a realistic opportunity to do so. Such 'ambush' cases would be caught by the government's proposed legislation, and should be considered as involving a significant exercise of the right to silence.

Accordingly, it is suggested that a suspect should be considered to exercise the right to silence in three categories of case:

(a)   where the suspect refuses to answer all questions;

(b)   where the suspect persists in refusing to answer particular questions relevant to his or her own involvement in an offence;

(c)   where a suspect answers questions but fails to disclose a defence which is later relied upon in court, where there was a realistic opportunity to disclose it.

In terms of this restrictive definition of significant silence, it seems probable that most of the pre-1993 studies would have overestimated the extent of silence. The earlier studies also suffer from a number of methodological problems which cast doubt on their reliability. Thus, studies conducted in the Metropolitan and West Yorkshire forces for the Home Office Working Group dealt with samples of interviews rather than suspects, thereby generating a risk of over-counting in relation to suspects who were silent during two or more interviews. Many of the studies have relied upon data collection by operational police officers with no guarantees that research instructions were understood or that adequate care was taken in completing the necessary questionnaires.

The appointment of the Royal Commission in 1991 provided an opportunity to clarify the notion of exercising the right to silence authoritatively and to quantify it. Unfortunately, the opportunity was largely squandered. Although the problem of definition is acknowledged, the Commission ultimately fall into the familiar trap of discussing silence without defining it. This loose thinking inevitably devalues the Commission's adopted estimates that silence is exercised by between 6 and 10% of suspects in the provinces and between 14 and 16% of suspects in the Metropolitan district.

The Commission also had the benefit of Zander and Henderson's Crown Court study (1993): perhaps the largest single piece of research on the English and Welsh criminal justice system. This study sampled every case tried in all Crown Courts (except three) over a two-week period, giving a total of 3,191 cases involving over 3,600 suspects. Lawyers involved in the study reported that between 11 and 13% of defendants had been silent in relation to all questions and that a further 9–10% had been 'significantly' silent in relation to some questions. These figures suggest that no less than 11% and no more than 23% of defendants exercised the right to silence. It is impossible to be more precise since there is no way of determining how many of the partially silent defendants exercised the right according to the definition offered above.

Whereas the Crown Court study dealt only with defendants tried in the Crown Court, research by ACPO, published contemporaneously with the Criminal Justice and Public Order Bill in December 1993, returns to the larger issue of silence among suspects in general. The study was conceived as a response to academic findings of low rates of silence, which were not accepted as realistic by the police service. The study is significant because of the size of the sample (3,600 suspects drawn from eight forces) and because the sample was collected as recently as September 1993.

ACPO found that 21.9% of suspects refused to answer some or all questions, with 10% completely silent. The study also confirms the link noted by other researchers between silence and legal advice, with 57% of legally advised suspects being totally or partially silent. In view of this linkage, it would have been expected that the rate of silence would rise following the redrafting of PACE Code of Practice C in 1991 which has had the effect of increasing the uptake of legal advice (Brown et al. 1992). However, it would be wise to treat the findings with some circumspection until fuller details of the research method are available. As noted above, data collection by many different operational officers poses problems. In particular, completing research forms would not be considered a high priority by busy officers and this might lead to inaccuracy or misinterpretation of the research instructions. ACPO indicate that the data forms were 'one per suspect'. It therefore appears that the survey avoids the risk of double-counting for suspects who are interviewed more than once, although it would be helpful if this were clarified.

The final reservation about the ACPO research is that it counts suspects who refuse to answer questions rather than suspects who exercise the right to silence. The 10% of suspects who decline all questions should clearly be considered as exercising the right. However, as argued above, without considering full transcripts of all interviews, it cannot be determined whether the 11.9% who decline some questions should be considered as exercising the right.

The 'problem' of silence

For ACPO silence is a problem because it 'is used to the advantage of practised criminals in the course of their "professional" business'. Presumably, the advantage referred to is the evasion of prosecution and conviction. If that is the problem then the ACPO study misleads by presenting figures on the rate of silence as if they were a measure of the problem. Other studies which have followed silence cases to their conclusion have found that about 50% of silent suspects are convicted, many after a guilty plea (Leng 1993; Zander and Henderson 1993; Yeo 1983). This suggests that the *starting-point* for estimating the size of the problem presented by silence should be at most half of ACPO's figure for silent suspects.

There are two reasons why the number of silent suspects who are not convicted should be considered as only the starting-point for estimating the extent of the silence problem. The first reason is that a significant proportion of such cases fail for reasons unconnected with silence. Typically a case will fail because of unavailability of a witness or through some defect in identification procedures (Leng 1993, pp. 27-9 and 39-40). Frequently in these cases the evidence is potentially strong and the suspect's silence is not in itself an impediment to prosecution.

The second reason why the problem of silence should not be measured in terms of the number of silent suspects avoiding conviction is that to do so would be to equate silence with guilt. This would be objectionable not only because it contradicts the presumption of innocence, but also because it flies in the face of the research evidence. McConville and Hodgson concluded that contrary to popular assumption, silence is normally explicable in terms of structural features of the criminal justice process rather than in terms of the guilt or innocence of the suspect. Thus, silence might be advised defensively by an unqualified legal adviser who is not confident about protecting the client's interests during interview. Silence may also be an advised tactic where the police have failed to disclose their evidence against a suspect or where interview techniques are designed to induce the suspect into unwitting incrimination (McConville and Hodgson 1993, ch. 6). There is also clear evidence that innocent suspects may use silence in order to shield another (Leng 1993, p. 20).

The message of these findings is that there are circumstances in which silence is a rational response for a suspect, whether guilty or innocent. If that is the case it is fair to assume that at least some silent suspects will be innocent. Overall, it is clear that the ACPO study is seriously misleading in its representation of the size of the problem of silence, and as such is likely to generate unrealistic expectations of what law reform could achieve.

The problem personified: the professional criminal

The ACPO research raises once again the spectre of the professional criminal who routinely exploits the right to silence to avoid his just deserts. Thus: 'As criminals become more experienced and professional they also become more proficient at exploiting the weakness of the judicial processes'. 'The reality is that [the right to silence] is a protection for hardened criminals.' ACPO supports these propositions by showing that 47% of suspects with five or more convictions exercise the right to silence, as against 15% of suspects with no criminal record.

Although the finding that suspects with criminal records exercise the right to silence much more frequently than others confirms earlier findings (Moston et al. 1993; Greer 1990, pp. 723–4), the finding does not imply that silence is a means of escaping conviction.

ACPO's figures on professional criminals must be assessed in the context of what is known about the practice of arrest and detention. The legal standard for arrest is reasonable suspicion. The codes of practice stress that there must be some objective basis for suspicion, and arrests based purely on criminal record are outlawed. However, the force of these provisions is weakened by three factors. First, the courts have stressed that suspicion involves no more than surmise and falls well short of evidence which tends to prove the offence (per Lord Devlin in *Hussien* v *Chong Fook Kam* [1970] AC 942). Secondly, real opportunities for judicial review of arrest and detention are negligible (Sanders 1988). Thirdly, research demonstrates that internal police reviews required by law operate only to legitimate earlier police decisions (McConville et al. 1991, pp. 40–7). The consequence is that police officers enjoy a virtually unlimited discretion in relation to arrest. Suspects may be arrested and detained where there is no direct evidence linking them to the offence, and the police continue to use criminal record as a criterion for arrest.

Thus, those with criminal records are far more likely to be arrested than other citizens and are the most likely to be arrested in circumstances where there is no objective evidence to link them to the offence. It is perhaps no surprise that the group of suspects who are most susceptible to repeated unjustified arrests are those most likely to exercise their right to silence. The fact that the majority of this group walk away from the police station without charge should not be seen as evidence of 'hardened criminals' 'thwarting justice' but rather as the natural and expected result of investigation policies which target known criminals and of a regime of ineffective regulation of policing which encourages speculative arrest on minimal evidence.

There is a further weakness in the ACPO case. On the one hand it is argued that professional criminals escape conviction by silence (the implication being that silence is indicative of guilt). On the other, figures are produced to support the claim that 'hardened criminals' routinely rely upon silence. But, if experienced criminals (like members of some terrorist organisations) rely on silence whatever the circumstances, the probative value of silence necessarily dissolves. The fact that the hardened criminal will remain silent, whether guilty or innocent, defeats any claim that for this group of suspects silence can be taken as evidence of guilt.

Testing the arguments for abolition

Among justifications offered for abolition of the right to silence are: the constitutional claim that it should be a citizen's duty to cooperate with the administration of justice; and the factual claim that the right is anachronistic because PACE and good police practice provide all necessary safeguards for the suspect (Easton 1991, ch. 3; compare Sanders 1988; Dixon 1990; McElree and Starmer 1992). However, the real motivation for abolition is the claim that abolition of the right would lead to the conviction of more guilty offenders. In turn this claim is based upon a series of assumptions about the current workings of the criminal process and about the likely effects of abolition.

The major assumptions underlying the case for abolition are:

(a)   that exercise of the right to silence enables criminals to withhold their defences and thereby gain unmerited acquittals by mounting ambush defences at trial which the prosecution are in no position to refute;

(b)   that by remaining silent, criminals hamper the investigation by denying the police the opportunity to test their defences in interview or by further investigation;

(c)   that more suspects would answer police questions if the present caution were to be replaced by a warning of the risks attached to remaining silent.

Research considered below casts doubt on the validity of these assumptions.

Ambush defences

Belief in the prevalence of ambush defences leading to unmerited acquittals has been the most powerful factor in the campaign for abolition of the right to silence (Criminal Law Revision Committee 1972, pp. 16–34; Hurd 1987; Home Office 1989). The recent Crown Court study provides some evidence to support that belief. Counsel reported that 'defences sprung on the prosecution at the last moment' featured in between 7 and 10% of Crown Court trials. However, significantly such cases were more likely to end in conviction than acquittal and prosecuting counsel reported that last-minute defences caused no particular difficulties in 40% of the cases in which they were raised (Zander and Henderson 1993, pp. 142–5). Thus, on the Crown Court study's figures, last-minute defences were raised and ended in acquittal in between 3.5 and 5% of trials. However, a closer consideration of the concept of an ambush defence suggests that even these modest figures may considerably overstate the problem.

Commentators who have discussed ambush defences have generally eschewed attempts at definition. However, it seems to be implicit in most accounts of the ambush problem, and also in the proposed legislative provision to deal with that problem, that ambush defences exhibit four characteristics:

(a)   that the defence is raised for the first time in court;

(b)   that the evidence or explanation on which the defence is based could have been given during police interrogation;

(c)   that the prosecution is hampered or prejudiced by the late disclosure of the defence; and

(d)   that the accused is advantaged by having more time to concoct or perfect a story and/or to prepare witnesses (Leng 1993, pp. 46–50).

An examination of the defences which may be raised in a criminal trial indicates that many defences cannot exhibit the characteristics of an ambush. Four commonly occurring categories of defence which it is argued could never amount to ambushes are considered below:

(a)   *Simple denials of an element of the offence*. Where such a defence is not supported by surprise evidence, it cannot involve prejudice to the prosecution, who must be prepared to prove all of the elements of the offence in any event.

(b)   *Defence based on pure legal argument*. This category cannot involve ambush since a suspect should not be expected to raise a purely legal issue during interview. Even where a legal adviser is present, it should not be expected that such issues should be raised at interview since the proper place for legal arguments is the court, not the police station. There should also be no question of prejudice to the prosecution since meeting an unexpected legal argument does not involve the same practical difficulties as dealing with unexpected evidence.

(c) *Defences based on the interpretation of the accused's answers in interview.* This is self-evidently a matter to be discussed at trial rather than in interview. However surprised the prosecution might be by a dispute about the meaning of the accused's words, there would be no prejudice since the only resource required to meet the defence would be the transcript which forms part of the prosecution's own evidence.

(d) *Challenge to the admissibility of alleged confession evidence.* In such cases the key factual issues relate to what occurred in the police station. Apart from the accused and perhaps also his or her legal adviser, the only witnesses will be police officers. Thus, the prosecution would have access to all relevant witnesses and would not be prejudiced by late notice of the defence.

This discussion suggests that apart from alibis, for which early disclosure has been a legal requirement since 1967, the scope for true ambush defences is very limited. It is certainly clear that many last-minute defences will not amount to ambushes. By equating last-minute defences with ambushes the Crown Court study would inevitably tend to overestimate the prevalence of ambush defences.

Research adopting the rigorous definition of ambush defences discussed above found that true ambushes occurred in no more than 5% of contested trials and probably in as few as 1.5% (Leng 1993, ch. 5). Interestingly, convictions were recorded in all cases involving an ambush or possible ambush. If these figures are representative, it suggests that acquittals arising from ambush defences are very rare indeed.

Does silence hamper investigations?

The claim that it would be advantageous to induce silent suspects to speak feeds on a stereotypical view of police work in which defences raised at interview are either skilfully undermined or subject to further investigation. This view is belied by the research. Baldwin (1993) found that:

> The image of police interviewers as professional, skilled and forceful interrogators scarcely matched the reality. More frequently officers emerged as nervous, ill at ease, and lacking in confidence.

In particular he found that some interviewers were badly prepared and asked apparently aimless and unfocused questions, whilst others failed to raise some matters vital to the proof of the offence in question. It is perhaps not surprising that the police are rarely successful in persuading suspects to deviate from their initial story (Moston et al. 1992, p. 38). Other researchers suggest that the police are successful in undermining defences raised at interview in between 5% (Leng 1993, pp. 61–4) and 7.5% (Baldwin 1993) of cases.[2]

Research also shows that, contrary to what might be expected, the police further investigate defences raised by the suspect at interview in only 19% of cases (Leng 1993, pp. 64–9). This figure is substantial but perhaps indicates that assumptions about the benefits which would flow from persuading silent suspects to speak are exaggerated. It must also be borne in mind that the figure of 19% does not represent a gain in the conviction of offenders since in many cases the fruit of further investigations was evidence to confirm the suspect's story.

Would reform induce silent suspects to speak?

It is assumed that by replacing the existing pre-interview caution with a warning about the risk of remaining silent, more suspects will decide to speak and legal advisers will advise silence less frequently. Both assumptions are open to doubt. As McConville and Hodgson have demonstrated, in many cases suspects remain silent or are advised to do so because of the perceived weakness of the case against them. Alternatively, silence may be a tactical response to a failure by the police to disclose what evidence they have against the suspect (McConville and Hodgson 1993, ch. 6). In either case, if the evidence is weak or is not believed to be strong, silence may be a rational choice for the suspect who realistically contemplates that the case will never reach court.

Even where the police are in possession of evidence against the suspect, silence would carry no risk unless and until the police disclosed their evidence in the course of interview. Whereas an inference might be drawn against a suspect who refused to answer a substantiated charge, there could be no question of drawing an inference from silence in the face of apparently

---

[2] In utilising these findings for the purposes of the right to silence debate, two reservations should be made. The first is that findings relating to suspects who choose to speak may not apply to silent suspects. Thus, it may be that suspects cooperate because they are confident of their ability to maintain their story under pressure, whilst the group of silent suspects includes those who either have no defence or whose story would crumble under cross-examination.

The second reservation is that the police and the Home Office have now rather belatedly addressed the deficiencies in interview techniques signalled by the recent studies. New national guidelines for interviewing have been devised and all interviewing officers will eventually be trained in their application (Home Office 1992a; 1992b). Although this process will take many years, the purpose of the guidelines is to improve the effectiveness of interviewing and if this occurs it may be expected that the police will become more successful in breaking down false stories. However, whatever the force of these reservations it must be accepted that at present there is little positive evidence to support the claim that persuading otherwise silent suspects to speak would benefit the prosecution in a large number of cases.

unfounded allegations or unfocused questions about the suspect's movement (Taylor of Gosforth 1994). It is also the view of the majority of the Royal Commission that whatever the weight of the evidence, changing the law is unlikely to induce experienced habitually silent suspects to speak (Royal Commission on Criminal Justice 1993, p. 54).

The experience of Singapore, which abolished the right to silence in 1976 along the lines proposed by the Criminal Law Revision Committee, lends support to the view that abolition is unlikely to decrease the numbers of suspects relying on silence. Comparing two similar samples of about 60 prosecutions in serious cases occurring before and after abolition, Yeo found that total silence was very rare and increased after abolition (Yeo 1983).[3]

Abolition and the risk of miscarriage

Arguments for retention of the right to silence have traditionally fallen into three categories: (a) arguments that the right is a necessary incident of adversarial justice (Dennis 1993); (b) constitutional arguments that the right protects citizens' interests in privacy and autonomy (Galligan 1988); and (c) arguments that abolition of the right would expose the suspect to the risk of wrongful conviction (Wood and Crawford 1989; Thornton et al. 1992; Royal Commission on Criminal Justice 1993, pp. 54–5). Whereas arguments in the first two categories proceed from statements of fundamental values which cannot be tested empirically, there is much research evidence which bears on the issue of whether abolition of the right would increase the risk of miscarriage of justice.

The primary risk for a suspect who is induced to speak is that the transcript which is the evidential product of the interview will not be the account which he would have given unprompted and may seriously misrepresent his position. The risk arises because the interview is not a generalised inquiry into an incident but rather is designed to achieve particular purposes. Although interviews have a variety of purposes, including in some cases establishing innocence, more frequently the aim is to build a case for the prosecution

---

[3]The Singapore research cannot provide a full picture of the incidence of silence because the sample consists only of prosecuted cases. It is possible that the right to silence was exercised by a significant number of suspects who were not prosecuted. In assessing the significance of the findings for the debate in England, it should also be borne in mind that it is not known how many of the Singapore suspects had access to legal advice. The statistical correlation between silence and legal advice is now well-established (although perhaps not fully understood). It seems unlikely that many suspects enjoyed custodial legal advice in Singapore in the mid 1970s whereas current English figures suggest that about 30 per cent of suspects receive some legal advice whilst in custody. Had similar levels of legal advice operated in Singapore at the time of the study, it is possible that this might have affected both the rate of silence and (in the post-abolition sample) the numbers of suspects who spoke only to avoid the possibility of adverse inferences being drawn against them.

(McConville et al. 1991). To this end the police employ a number of techniques, including control of the agenda of the interview, supply to the accused of the story which they wish to hear, and supply of the terminology in which they wish to hear it. In extreme cases this can lead to vulnerable suspects adopting the story suggested by the police (Gudjonsson 1992). Perhaps more commonly, suspects are prejudiced: by agreeing to propositions which they may not fully understand, by inadvertently adopting terminology suggestive of guilt, and by failure to fully develop and explain their defence (McConville et al. 1991, ch. 4; Leng 1993, pp. 55–8; Evans 1993).

In view of the potency of admissions at interview in producing guilty verdicts (whether by plea or following a trial) it is not surprising that some suspects and/or their legal advisers seek to avoid these risks by maintaining silence in interview and by saving any defence for the more controlled environment of the courtroom.

If the right to silence is abolished as proposed by the government, risks willl also attend the suspect who chooses to keep silent. The obvious primary risk is that silence would be wrongly treated as evidence of guilt (McElree and Starmer 1992; Jackson 1993). Although under the proposed legislation the defendant would have the opportunity to refute the inference of guilt by explaining his or her reasons for silence, this in turn may carry risks. As McConville and Hodgson (1993) have shown, in many cases the reason is dislike or lack of respect for the police rooted in earlier dealings with them. It may serve the defendant little for the jury to discover that he or she hates the police or has been a frequent visitor to police stations. There is a real risk that such evidence, suggestive of bad character, may distract the jury from their only task which is to decide whether there is sufficient evidence that the defendant had committed a particular crime.

A secondary risk is that the defendant who has remained silent in the police station will be inhibited from running his defence in court. Under the proposed legislation the jury could infer that a defence was fabricated if it was raised for the first time in court. Since it is a short step from inferring that a defence is fabricated to inferring guilt of the crime charged, the defendant might be well-advised to not disclose his or her defence and rely upon the prosecution failing to prove their case. This is particularly likely to occur where the defence is based solely on the accused's own testimony: although as a matter of fact the lack of supporting evidence is as likely to result from inadequate legal aid and poor preparation by defence lawyers as from the inherent weakness of the defence (Baldwin 1992; McConville et al. 1994).

Revolution and counter-revolution in police investigations

The last few years have witnessed a concerted attempt to professionalise the process of investigation with a view to improving the quality of evidence presented in court. What is in effect a revolution in police investigations was inspired by a recognition of the fallibility of traditional confession evidence and a desire to clarify and formalise the rights of suspects. The revolution was instigated by the report of the Royal Commission on Criminal Procedure in 1981 and PACE and the codes of practice which followed it. It has been carried forward by an increasingly interventionist stance by the courts (Feldman 1990; Birch 1989), by the redrafting of the code of practice on detention and interrogation in 1991 (Wolchover and Heaton-Armstrong 1991) and by the willingness of the Home Office and the police service to rethink the proper approach to police interviewing (McGurk et al. 1993).

The thrust of the reforms has been to reduce reliance on less credible forms of evidence. Thus, police interviewing for the purpose of collecting evidence should now be reserved for the police station and will normally be recorded on tape.[4] Untaped alleged admissions may still be admissible as evidence but only where made spontaneously or in response to limited permissible questioning (*R* v *Cox* (1992) 96 Cr App R 464; *R* v *Weekes* (1992) 97 Cr App R 222). Alleged untaped admissions will not be admissible as evidence unless they have been recorded in writing at the earliest opportunity and shown to the suspect for verification or comment (PACE Code C, paras 11.5 to 11.13; *R* v *Chung* (1990) 92 Cr App R 314).

A benefit of the reforms has been to reduce the opportunities for 'verballing' by police officers, and for allegations of verballing by defendants, leading to more guilty pleas and shortened trials.

These developments are now threatened by the government's proposals which in certain circumstances would remove the suspect's right to silence on the street. Under clauses 29 and 30 of the Criminal Justice and Public Order Bill, adverse inferences may be drawn against a suspect who fails to account for incriminating objects, substances or marks, or for his or her presence near the scene of a crime. The effects of these provisions will amount to no less than a counter-revolution in police investigations. Officers will once again be encouraged to undertake substantial questioning on the street after arrest. Since there is no requirement that arrests should be tape-recorded[5] it seems very likely that the new provision will generate disputes in court about what was and was not said on the street, giving rise to more and longer trials at great expense to the public purse (Bridges 1994).

The new provisions will invite police corruption (or allegations of police corruption) and create multiple risks for the suspect. Thus, where other

---

[4]Research indicates that significant interchanges between police and suspects still frequently take place outside the station (Moston and Stephenson 1993) and concern remains about the extent to which such interchanges may influence the content of the formal recorded interview (Leng 1994).
[5]Compare the recommendation of the Royal Commission on Criminal Justice that more use should be made of tape recorders at the time of arrest (1993, pp. 27–8).

evidence is not forthcoming, the police could claim that a question was asked which the suspect refused to answer, or could deny that the suspect had responded to a question. For the suspect who is coerced into responding before receiving legal advice and before becoming aware of the suspicion against him or her, there is a real danger of inadvertent incrimination.

Conclusion

The appointment of the Royal Commission in 1991 promised an era of rational development in criminal justice in which reform would follow research. With the publication of the Criminal Justice and Public Order Bill in 1993 it became apparent that that promise was not to be fulfilled. An examination of the provisions on the right to silence indicates not only that few of the lessons of research have been heeded but also that the government is prepared to throw away real improvements in police investigations and prosecutions in pursuit of the nebulous aim of getting tough on law and order.

Many who have been involved in the development of criminal justice policy will be disappointed by the reforms to come. However, that disappointment will be shared by those in government and elsewhere who have high expectations of what the reforms will deliver. At most abolition of the right to silence will lead to conviction in a very small proportion of cases which otherwise would have ended in no prosecution or acquittal. But that benefit will have its cost in terms of extended trials and more miscarriages of justice.

References

ACPO (1993), *The Right of Silence: Briefing Paper* (London: Association of Chief Police Officers of England, Wales and Northern Ireland).
Baldwin, J. (1992), *The Role of Legal Representatives at Police Stations* (Royal Commission Criminal Justice Research Study No. 3) (London: HMSO).
Baldwin, J. (1993), 'Police interview techniques', *British Journal of Criminology*, vol. 33, pp. 325–52.
Birch, D. (1989), 'The PACE hots up: confessions and confusion under the 1984 Act', *Criminal Law Review*, pp. 95–116.
Bridges, L. (1994), 'The silence about what it will cost', *Parliamentary Brief* (February), p. 8.
Brown, D., Ellis, T., and Larcombe, K. (1992), *Changing the Code: Police Detention under the Revised PACE Codes of Practice* (Home Office Research Study No. 129) (London: HMSO).
Criminal Law Revision Committee (1972), *Eleventh Report: Evidence (General)* (Cmnd 4991) (London: HMSO).

Dennis, I. (1993), '*Instrumental protection or human right?: the fall and rise (?) of the privilege against self-incrimination*'. Paper delivered at the International Conference on Criminal Procedure and the Rights of the Accused, Jerusalem, December 1993.

Dixon, D. (1990), 'Politics, research and symbolism in criminal justice: the right to silence and the Police and Criminal Evidence Act', *Anglo-American Law Review*, vol. 20, p. 27.

Easton, S. (1991), *The Right to Silence* (Aldershot: Avebury).

Evans, R. (1993) *The Conduct of Police Interviews with Juveniles* (Royal Commission on Criminal Justice Research Study No. 8) (London: HMSO).

Feldman, D. (1990) 'Regulating treatment of suspects in police stations: judicial interpretation of provisions in the Police and Criminal Evidence Act 1984' *Criminal Law Review*, pp. 452–71.

Galligan, D. J. (1988), 'The right to silence reconsidered', *Current Legal Problems 1988*, p. 69.

Greer, S. (1990), 'The right to silence: a review of the current debate', *Modern Law Review*, vol. 53, p. 709.

Gudjonsson, G. (1992), *The Psychology of Interrogations, Confessions and Testimony* (Chichester: Wiley).

Home Office (1989), *Report of the Working Group on the Right to Silence* (London: Home Office).

Home Office (1992a), *A Guide to Interviewing* (Harrogate: Home Office Central Planning & Training Unit).

Home Office (1992b), *The Interviewer's Rule Book* (Harrogate: Home Office Central Planning & Training Unit).

Hurd, D. (1987), Police Foundation Lecture, 30 July 1987.

Irving, B. and McKenzie, I. (1989), *Police interrogation: the Effects of the Police and Criminal Evidence Act 1984* (London: Police Foundation).

Jackson, J. (1990), 'Recent developments in Northern Ireland', in S. Greer and R. Morgan, *The Right to Silence Debate* (Bristol: Bristol and Bath Centre for Criminal Justice), pp. 44–52.

Jackson, J. (1991) 'Curtailing the right of silence: lessons from Northern Ireland', *Criminal Law Review*, pp. 404–15.

Jackson, J. (1993), 'Inferences from silence: from common law to common sense', *Northern Ireland Legal Quarterly*, vol. 44, pp. 103–12.

LAG (1991), *LAG's Submission to the Royal Commission on Criminal Justice* (London: Legal Action Group).

Law Society (1992), *Evidence to the Royal Commission on Criminal Justice* (London: Law Society).

Lawton, F. (1987), 'How the right to silence has blocked convictions', *Independent*, 28 August.

Leng, R. (1993), *The Right to Silence in Police Interrogation: a Study of Some of the Issues underlying the Debate* (Royal Commission on Criminal Justice Research Study No. 10) (London: HMSO).

Leng, R. (1994), 'A recipe for miscarriage: the Royal Commission and informal interviews', in McConville, M. and Bridges, L. (eds), *Criminal Justice in Crisis* (London: Edward Elgar).

McConville, M., and Baldwin, J. (1981), *Courts, Prosecution and Conviction* (Oxford: Clarendon Press).

McConville, M., Sanders, A., and Leng, R. (1991), *The Case for the Prosecution* (London: Routledge).

McConville, M. and Hodgson, J. (1993), *Custodial Legal Advice and the Right to Silence* (Royal Commission on Criminal Justice Research Study No. 16) (London: HMSO).

McConville, M., Hodgson, J., and Bridges, L. (1994), *Standing Accused* (Oxford: OUP).

McElree, F., and Starmer, K. (1992), 'The right to silence', in C. Walker and K. Starmer (eds), *Justice in Error* (London: Blackstone), pp. 58–74.

McGurk, B., Carr, J., and McGurk, D. (1993), *Investigative Interviewing Courses for Police Officers: an Evaluation* (Police Research Series Paper No. 4) (London: Home Office Police Research Group).

McKenzie, I. and Irving, B. (1988), 'The right to silence' *Policing*, vol. 4, p. 88.

Mark, R. (1973), *Minority Verdict* (London: BBC Publications).

Moston, S., and Stephenson, G.M. (1993), *The Questioning and Interviewing of Suspects outside the Police Station* (Royal Commission on Criminal Justice Research Study No. 22) (London: HMSO).

Moston, S., Stephenson, G.M., and Williamson, T. (1992), 'The effects of case characteristics on suspect behaviour during questioning', *British Journal of Criminology*, vol. 32, pp. 23–40.

Moston, S., Stephenson, G.M., and Williamson, T. (1993), 'The incidence, antecedents and consequences of the use of the right to silence during police questioning', *Criminal Behaviour and Mental Health*, vol. 3, pp. 30–47.

Royal Commission on Criminal Justice (1993), *Report* (Cm 2263) (London: HMSO).

Royal Commission on Criminal Procedure (1981), *Report* (Cmnd 8092) (London: HMSO).

Ruddell, G. (1990), 'A summary of recent judicial decisions in Northern Ireland', in S. Greer and R. Morgan (eds), ght to Silence Debate (Bristol: Bristol and Bath Centre for Criminal Justice), pp. 53–9.

Sanders, A. (1988), 'Rights, remedies and the Police and Criminal Evidence Act', *Criminal Law Review*, p. 802.

Taylor of Gosforth, Lord (1994), 'The Tom Sargant Memorial Lecture', *New Law Journal*, vol. 144, pp. 125–9.

Thornton, P., Mallalieu, A., and Scrivener, A. (1992), *Justice on Trial*, Report of the Independent Civil Liberty Panel on Criminal Justice (London: Civil Liberties Trust).

Wolchover, D. and Heaton-Armstrong, A. (1991) 'The questioning Code revamped' *Criminal Law Review*, pp. 232-41.

Wood, J. and Crawford, A. (1989) *The Right to Silence: The Case for Retention* (London: Civil Liberties Trust).

Yeo, M. (1983), 'Diminishing the right to silence: the Singapore experience', *Criminal Law Review*, pp. 89–101.

Zander, M. (1979), 'The investigation of crime: a study of cases tried at the Old Bailey', *Criminal Law Review*, p. 203.

Zander, M. (1993a), 'A note of dissent', in Royal Commission on Criminal Justice, *Report* (London: HMSO), pp. 221–35.

Zander, M. (1993b), 'How will the right of silence be abolished?', *New Law Journal*, vol. 143, pp. 1716–18.

Zander, M., and Henderson, P. (1993), *The Crown Court Study* (Royal Commission on Criminal Justice Research Study No. 19) (London: HMSO).

2

The Wrong Message at the Wrong Time? The Present State of Investigative Practice

Mike Maguire

Introduction

The research on criminal investigations carried out by Clive Norris and myself for the Royal Commission (Maguire and Norris 1992) was concerned with the general control and supervision of investigations in different contexts, with particular emphasis upon factors which might increase or reduce the risk of police malpractice or serious investigative errors — and hence miscarriages of justice. This, I note — despite its centrality to the cases which led to the setting up of the Royal Commission in the first place — is an issue which seems to have taken more of a back seat as the debate arising from the Commission's report has developed.

The bottom line of what I have to say is that the move towards abolition of the right to silence is a retrograde step, not only on grounds of principle, but because it appears to me a wrong message to send to the police service at a time when it has begun to make serious efforts to tackle long-standing problems in its organisation and its approach to crime investigation. In particular, it is a message which may undermine the current willingness of the police to attempt to reduce their traditional heavy reliance upon admissions and to seek safer forms of evidence. I shall also argue that the process of change in investigative practice is as yet only in its infancy, and numerous practical problems have to be overcome before one can take seriously the argument that the right to silence is no longer necessary.

The argument against a right to silence in investigative interviews is clearly stronger in inquisitorial, as opposed to adversarial, systems of justice where interviews are independent of the police and suspects are made fully aware of the evidence against them. However, the term 'inquisitorial' has sometimes been used in a much more limited sense, to support arguments put forward for abolition in this country, notably in the call for a 'right to comment' on a suspect's silence, made in the police evidence submitted to the Royal Commission (Police Service 1991). This focused upon the greater safeguards available to suspects since the Police and Criminal Evidence Act 1984 (PACE) and also included an assertion of the aim of the police to make investigations, particularly interviews in custody, 'more inquisitorial' in the sense of constituting a 'search for the truth', though still taking place within the context of an adversarial legal system. In this paper, I shall leave aside the philosophical question of whether efforts to move towards an inquisitorial style of police investigation would alone justify in an adversarial system a duty to answer questions. Rather, I shall question the empirical base of the argument, in the light of research by myself and others into the practice of police investigation and the cultural and organisational context in which it takes place.

A redundant safeguard?

The Police Service, in its written evidence, argued that courts should be allowed to take into account accused persons' failure to answer police questions on the following grounds. First, suspects were said to be properly protected by the well-known reforms of custody records, tape recording of interviews, access to legal advice, and so on, making the further safeguard of a right to silence redundant. This is very like what Stephen Greer (1990), in a valuable pre-Commission article on the topic, called the 'exchange-abolitionist' argument: the right to silence can be given up as a quid pro quo for proper legal protections. Secondly, police investigations were asserted in practice to have become more akin to a 'search for the truth': under the influence of PACE, far more evidence was now produced prior to arrest, and the use of interviews as 'fishing expeditions' was no longer possible. Thirdly, the general assertion was made that police investigations were now more 'open'. In these circumstances, it was argued, it is reasonable to expect suspects to answer questions put to them at the time, rather than reserve their defence until a court appearance. Consequently, the prosecution should have a 'right to comment' on a defence not brought up during the police interview. This fits with more general comments made by many police commentators in recent years, to the effect that investigations have become more 'ethical' and are better controlled and supervised (see, for example, Williamson 1993 and chapter 7 below).

Now, unlike some critics, I have become convinced that there have been improvements — indeed, quite considerable improvements — in all the above aspects of investigative practice over the last few years, not least because of the very existence of the Royal Commission. However, I also believe there is a very long way to go and that fundamental problems remain. I shall illustrate this briefly with a few general points arising from research.

First of all, let us take the issue of 'evidence before arrest'. From what I have seen, during a considerable amount of contact with the police service (particularly the CID), it is still very common for people to be arrested before much evidence has been gathered, and confessions are still regarded as an essential element in obtaining convictions. In many forces, the majority of arrests are made by uniformed officers, who quite commonly pass the suspect on to a CID officer for interview. The latter's principal objective, openly acknowledged by all those involved, is to elicit a clear admission: other evidence is often unlikely to be sufficient in itself to secure a conviction.

In the real world, the scenario in which detailed forensic, witness or physical evidence is systematically collected before arrest, followed by a carefully planned interview in which all the evidence is put to the suspect, is relatively rare, confined principally to proactive 'target' operations and to reactive investigations into major offences, usually carried out by teams of detectives working from an incident room. In proactive investigations carried out by central specialist squads, officers are more likely to have the luxuries of relatively uninterrupted concentration on one case at a time, less pressure from senior officers to produce results in the form of large numbers of arrests, and easier access to resources such as surveillance capabilities which facilitate the production of more solid evidence. At subdivisional level, however, even in cases handled solely by the CID, the basic pattern of investigation is quite different. Detective activity is dominated by routine work on heavy case-loads, constant juggling of cases to meet immediate demands and unforeseen developments, and pressure to keep senior officers happy by maintaining an acceptable clear-up rate. Work at this level was aptly described many years ago by Sanders (1977) as 'a mosaic of tasks': the work is reactive in every sense, and decisions to arrest are, inevitably, made in a hasty and relatively unplanned manner as circumstances dictate.

Nevertheless, an important set of reservations must be added to the above picture as quite serious efforts are currently being made, both within police forces and by bodies concerned with the monitoring and inspection of the police, to bring about major changes in investigative practice. The Audit Commission (1993), for example, has recently added its weight to the advocacy of 'intelligence-driven' models of investigation, whereby local CID offices 'target the crime, not the criminal' and make more use of proactive techniques involving surveillance, informants, crime pattern analysis and computerised intelligence systems. One manifestation of this approach is the growth of dedicated force surveillance squads, which can be 'hired out' to local police divisions to gather observational evidence on 'targeted criminals' (and, ideally, to 'catch them in the act'). Another example is the sustained large-scale drive, based on proactive methods, against particular types of offender, perhaps best illustrated by the anti-burglary 'Operation Bumblebee' in London. Target operations of these kinds, augmented by photographic or video records derived from surveillance, often produce sufficient evidence to convict offenders without the need for confession evidence. They are broadly supported by the Association of Chief Police Officers, the Home Office and HM Inspectorate of Constabulary, and by many local police managers who agree that 'this is the way forward'.

Such developments, which form part of a general trend towards 'crime management' systems (as opposed to the traditional *ad hoc* reaction to events as they come to notice), certainly encourage the search for alternative forms of evidence and facilitate better preparation of cases before arrests are made, but they are (a) very expensive and (b) involve major changes in police culture and organisational structure. Consequently, they often give rise to protracted in-force battles in which, for example, proponents of a dedicated surveillance squad have unsuccessfully sought the manpower and equipment necessary to set it up properly. Even in forces where such problems have been overcome, arrests obtained in this way usually constitute only a very small proportion of the total. The achievement of a wholesale shift of resources and activity in this direction is, at best, a long-term project.

A second way in which it has been claimed that reforms have greatly increased suspects' protection — and hence reduced the justification for allowing them to remain silent without penalty — is through the safeguard against unfair 'fishing expeditions' which is supposedly afforded by the gatekeeper role of the custody officer. However, the notion that custody officers always carefully question arresting officers about their reasons for bringing in suspects and do not allow detention for questioning without sufficient reason, seems from all the evidence available to remain something of a myth. In the sample of over 2,000 arrests examined by Morgan et al. (1990), only one case was found of detention not being accepted by a custody officer — and that was because the person concerned had suffered a stroke. In common with several other researchers in this area — some of whom have further argued that custody officers sometimes collude with investigators by using ploys to deny suspects their full rights (see, for example, McConville et al. 1991) — Morgan et al. concluded that the notion of custody officer as effective gatekeeper is largely a 'presentational fig-leaf'. Whether many custody officers deliberately bend the rules to gain unfair advantages over suspects for their colleagues' benefit is debatable, but there are other, more mundane, reasons why they may be inclined to allow, rather than refuse, detention in borderline cases. These include simple pressure of time. And, not least, it is against the prevailing police culture of supporting colleagues for a custody officer to say to an officer in front of a suspect, 'There is not enough evidence here to warrant detention' — a statement which implicitly questions the officer's professional judgement.

The police argument for the abolition of a right to silence in interviews also includes the claim that the conduct of interviews themselves is now sufficiently 'professional', as well as regulated by tape recording and the presence of solicitors, to make the 'extra' guarantee of a right to silence unnecessary. It is asserted, for example, that interviewing skills are generally of a high standard, that interviews are well structured, that questions are properly put, and so on. There is, however, ample evidence that much interviewing is of poor quality and that there are still major training needs in this area. For example, Baldwin and Moloney's (1992) research for the Royal Commission documents many rambling and repetitive interviews, unfair and irrelevant questions, and attempts to badger suspects into concurring with police versions of events. While, again, it can rightly be claimed that serious efforts are being made by the police to improve the quality of interviewing, this, too, is a long-term project and one would wish to see clear evidence of its success before accepting it as a valid argument in favour of removing the right to silence.

Another problematic area is the poor quality of legal advice experienced by many suspects in police stations. Research studies conducted specifically for the Royal Commission (McConville and Hodgson 1993; Baldwin 1992), as well as a large-scale study shortly to be published (McConville et al. 1994), provide strong evidence that legal advice is often given by unqualified people, that solicitors often know little about the police case when they go into the interview, and that it is not uncommon for them to fail to intervene in questioning if it begins to become oppressive. If one adds to this (a) the fact that the majority of those questioned do not request or receive legal advice anyway, (b) the finding mentioned above that custody officers sometimes actively discourage suspects from requesting legal advice, and (c) the point that there are opportunities for police officers to engage in some form of negotiation with suspects before they enter the police station about what may be said in the interview (see, for example, Moston and Stephenson 1993; Maguire and Norris 1992), it becomes difficult to sustain the argument that interviews have now become sufficiently well conducted and regulated to justify removing the ancient safeguard of a right to silence.

The prevention of malpractice

I turn now to the specific problem of the prevention of malpractice — an issue which many thought should be fundamental to the concerns of the Royal Commission. Our study, it should be noted, was not aimed at discovering how much malpractice takes place — perhaps an impossible task — but to look at the potential for malpractice in specific situations and to assess the effectiveness of the systems in place to prevent it.

The problem of investigative malpractice can be illuminated first of all by an awareness of the history of the CID and its traditional separation from the uniform branch. Its history has been marked by periodic scandals, often followed by a sudden cleansing of the stables — one of the most dramatic being the enforced early retirement of many London detectives at the behest of the Metropolitan Police Commissioner, Robert Mark, in the 1970s (Cox et al. 1977). To explain why problems of corruption and malpractice have emerged so often, one has to look at both the special nature of CID work (which involves officers in frequent unsupervised contact with people who pursue a criminal lifestyle) and the élite status which CID officers have traditionally enjoyed (Hobbs 1988; Maguire and Norris 1992). One has also to consider the CID culture which grew up over many years, aided by the fact that, until relatively recently, it was common for officers to spend large parts of their careers uninterruptedly in the CID — even in one particular detective squad — and for the selection and appointment of detectives to be heavily influenced by career CID managers (see, for example, Kaye 1991). The extra pay which could be earned by detectives, and the perception of a CID posting as a form of promotion, created strong incentives for those appointed to the department to make every effort to remain in it. Dislike of the idea of being returned to uniform duties was still very common among the detective constables with whom we spent time. It was reflected in remarks such as, 'If you're not careful you'll be back on the streets in a pointed hat', or the notice one DC recalls pinned upon an office wall, 'A sus a day keeps the helmet away'.

This slogan also reflects the price of maintaining CID status — a constant 'pressure to perform'. Despite changes in recent years, the CID clearly remains highly results-orientated: what matters above all else — the very *raison d'être* of the detective branch — is to arrest criminals. The pressure that this creates for individual officers takes a variety of forms, depending upon the type of unit to which they are posted. For example, in a high-profile murder investigation there may be enormous media and financial pressure upon the officer leading the inquiry to expedite matters and make an arrest, while at a local level there may be less intense, but continuing, pressure upon sergeants and constables to improve a below-average clear-up rate. But whatever form they may take, the common factors throughout the CID are high expectations, hard work and often long hours.

The relationship between this pressure and malpractice is a complex one, but most known examples have certainly shown a connection. The public outrage and desire for revenge produced by major terrorist offences undoubtedly contributed to some of the gross violations of suspects' rights which have been well documented in infamous miscarriage cases, while at a more mundane level, pressure to maintain clear-up rates in the face of both greatly increased recorded crime rates and more clearly defined limits to their official powers, has made it difficult for detectives to satisfy their managers without sometimes engaging in at least minor forms of rule bending, especially in efforts to secure confession evidence. Attention has also been drawn to the phenomenon of 'noble cause' malpractice, where evidence against people 'known' to have committed offences has been 'enhanced' (a process sometimes referred to by police officers as 'gilding the lily') in order to guarantee a conviction. This has been associated in extreme cases with obsessionally hard-working officers, who have come to believe that they have a 'mission' to 'take villains off the street' and that procedural rules put unnecessary barriers in the way of the achievement of an aim which benefits society (see, for example, Short 1991).

Such problems and dangers, of course, have long been recognised within the police service and various internal mechanisms, including training, supervision and an elaborate complaints system, are partly designed to deter individuals from succumbing to pressures or temptations. (Some of these mechanisms, it should be noted, have multiple purposes, including the promotion of discipline, hard work and efficiency, as well as deterrence against dishonesty in areas such as expense and overtime claims.) However, their effectiveness in preventing malpractice has often been open to question, as has the commitment of police managers and supervisors to the prevention of at least minor forms of malpractice, so long as these remain hidden from external view. Skilful rule bending, of course, is likely to increase effectiveness in crime detection, which is important to senior, as well as to junior, officers in terms of career progression.

One regulatory mechanism at which we looked specifically in our study was that of supervision within the CID. In common with Baldwin and Moloney (1992) and Irving and Dunnighan (1993), we found that, in practice, supervision was often minimal and was not geared primarily to the prevention of malpractice. Monitoring of detective constables' activity through routines such as checking pocketbooks was generally seen by detective sergeants as a means of 'ensuring that people are working', rather than as a means of preventing breaches of suspects' rights.

These findings reflect the view that detective sergeants have traditionally taken of their role, as 'part of a team' rather than as supervisors *per se*:

'super-DCs' as some have described them. They often carry their own case-loads and work in partnership with constables, leaving little time to look in detail at what others are doing. We described the predominant style of supervision as 'charismatic' as opposed to 'bureaucratic': a style which emphasises leadership, team motivation and the encouragement of initiative and productivity, rather than strict conformity to procedural rules. Such a style of supervision puts a high premium upon trust — it was generally regarded as invidious and counter-productive to check upon people too often. This, it should be stressed, is not simply a matter of close personal relationships within the police. It reflects the view — grounded in experience — that to do their job effectively, detectives need to use initiative and a degree of autonomy (we were frequently told, indeed, that CID selection criteria include 'the ability to work without supervision').

In sum, the charismatic mode of supervision has considerable advantages from an operational viewpoint and, if sergeants are of high quality, does not preclude subtle means of finding out whether constables are observing suspects' rights. Problems, of course, may arise either if sergeants are not perceptive or, worse, if their hands-on involvement in cases and loyalty to the team leads them to ignore or even to collude in malpractice. If this occurs, it is possible for standards to slide rapidly, with no effective mechanism to correct the slide (Kaye 1991; Baldwin and Moloney 1992).

Concluding remarks

The main thrust of my argument is that the problems I have referred to are complex and deep-seated and one cannot expect lasting solutions without a sustained period of genuine commitment to reform. The good news is that there have recently been many signs of such commitment within the police service, stimulated in no small measure by the shock waves from the spate of miscarriage cases which came to light in the late 1980s. The bad news, I suggest, is that the necessary momentum is unlikely to be sustained.

I have no time for a detailed account of the positive developments which are taking place, but a few examples may be given. First, many forces have adopted rules which restrict the length of time that officers can serve continuously in the CID; make selection and recruitment into the CID a more open process with greater 'uniform' influence; and/or stipulate at least a temporary return to uniform duties on promotion. The organisational structure of the CID, too, has been undergoing major changes: it is now common for local CID offices to be solely under the line management and financial control of the (uniformed) divisional commander, rather than answering to CID managers in headquarters. Some of these changes, it is true, have been motivated more by reasons of efficiency and the fashionable devolution of budgets to local units, than by a desire to alter investigative practice. Nevertheless, they do already appear to be reducing the insularity of the CID by increasing the interchange of personnel and promoting more joint working between detectives and uniform officers. In the longer term, deliberately or not, they could play a part in a lasting transformation in CID culture and working practices.

Secondly, as Tom Williamson describes in chapter 7, there have been significant reforms in CID training programmes, including the promotion of concepts such as ethical interviewing (see also Williamson 1993). Supervisory structures, too, have seen changes, such as the system introduced in the Metropolitan Police District as part of the Crime Investigation Priority Project, whereby each detective sergeant is given full responsibility for (and accountability for the activities of) a specific group of detective constables and works with a clear job description emphasising the supervisory role (Gibb-Gray 1990). In our report for the Royal Commission (Maguire and Norris 1992) we suggested various other reforms aimed at closer internal monitoring of detective activity, including the institution of independent 'quality control units' (with the power to conduct random inspections of investigative documents and tapes) and the appointment of 'PACE officers', who would be attached to major investigations with a duty to monitor compliance with the codes of practice. These, too, have received serious consideration.

Finally, I would single out two developments which, in the long term, could prove most important of all. First, the widespread efforts to make more use of proactive methods of investigation, which — although certainly not without their dangers, especially in dealings with informants — generally produce sounder evidence than investigations which rely primarily upon admissions. And secondly, signs of a willingness among police managers (paralleled, again, in the Home Office police divisions and in the Inspectorate) to attach less importance to the clear-up rate, and to raise the profile of the concept of 'quality' as a criterion of assessment. Suggestions have been made that individual officers' work should be judged as much by its adherence to norms of 'good practice' as by its output in terms of arrests and detections. This, I have to say, remains at present largely at the level of rhetoric, and there is a great deal of cultural resistance to overcome. However, if the concept can be operationalised, with real rewards given for work demonstrating 'quality', it too could have significant long-term consequences.

Unfortuantely, it has to be stressed that, laudable as they are, all the above reforms are still only in their infancy. They are by no means so well established, nor is the commitment to them by the police service so secure, that one can be confident that the momentum will be maintained. Priorities in the police service change quickly, and are strongly influenced by the political 'mood'. Despite the current openness of the police, in the aftermath of the Royal Commission, to suggestions for reform, and despite the real signs of progress mentioned, I have serious worries about the effects of the very different messages that the government has begun to send out. Some of these messages are at a general level, signalling 'tougher' approaches to crime and the treatment of offenders. If such messages were accompanied by firm statements of commitment to fair and open investigations and the protection of suspects' rights, there would be less reason to fear backtracking by the police from commitment to investigative reform. However, not only are statements of this kind virtually absent, but specific proposals appear to send out quite opposite messages.

The plan to abolish the right to silence is one such example. Ignoring the recommendations of successive Royal Commissions, this seems to me to have the potential to undermine seriously some of the internal police reforms I have outlined. It could have the effect of encouraging a reversal of the move away from reliance upon confessions as the central plank of investigative strategy. Rather than encouraging detectives to seek other forms of evidence — a strategy which is more difficult and challenging and demands more resources, but is more likely to deliver justice — it returns the focus to the interview room, with all the attendant dangers of oppressive questioning, false confessions, and so on. While the memory of the major miscarriages of justice still remains fresh, these dangers may not be as strong as they once were. However, history suggests that, without radical reform, it is only a matter of time before old habits return and the cycle repeats itself.

References

Audit Commission (1993), *Helping with Enquiries: Tackling Crime Effectively* (London: Audit Commission).

Baldwin, J. (1992), *The Role of Legal Representatives at the Police Station* (Royal Commission on Criminal Justice Research Study No. 2) (London: HMSO).

Baldwin, J., and Moloney, T. (1992), *The Supervision of Investigations in Serious Criminal Cases* (Royal Commission on Criminal Justice Research Study No. 4) (London: HMSO).

Cox, B., Shirley, J., and Short, M. (1977), *The Fall of Scotland Yard* (Harmondsworth: Penguin).

Gibb-Gray, B. (1990), 'Reorganising crime investigation', *Policing*, vol. 6, pp. 355–62.

Greer, S. (1990), 'Background to the debate', in S. Greer and R. Morgan (eds), *The Right to Silence Debate* (Bristol: Bristol and Bath Centre for Criminal Justice).

Hobbs, R. (1988), *Doing the Business* (Oxford: Clarendon Press).

Irving, B., and Dunninghan, C. (1993), *Human Factors in the Quality Control of CID Investigations* (Royal Commission on Criminal Justice Research Study No. 21) (London: HMSO).

Kaye, T. (1991), *Unsafe and Unsatisfactory? Report of the Independent Inquiry Into the Working Practices of the West Midlands Serious Crimes Squad* (Civil Liberties Trust).

Maguire, M., and Norris, C. (1992), *The Conduct and Supervision of Criminal Investigations* (Royal Commission on Criminal Justice Research Study No. 5) (London: HMSO).

McConville, M., and Hodgson, J. (1993) *Custodial Legal Advice and the Right to Silence* (Royal Commission on Criminal Justice Research Study No. 16) (London: HMSO).

McConville, M., Hodgson, J., Bridges, L., and Pavlovic, A. (1994), *Standing Accused* (Oxford: Clarendon Press).

McConville, M., Sanders, A., and Leng, R. (1991), *The Case for the Prosecution* (London: Routledge).

Morgan, R., Reiner, R., and McKenzie, I. (1990), *Police Powers and Policy: A Study of the Work of Custody Officers*. Final Report to the Economic and Social Research Council (unpublished).

Moston, S., and Stephenson, G.M. (1993), *The Questioning and Interviewing of Suspects outside the Police Station* (Royal Commission on Criminal Justice Research Study No. 22) (London: HMSO).

Police Service (1991), *Evidence from the Police Service of England and Wales to the Royal Commission on Criminal Justice* (unpublished).

Sanders, W. (1977), *Detective Work: A Study of Criminal Investigations* (New York: Free Press).

Short, M. (1991), *Lundy: the Destruction of London's Finest Detective* (London: Grafton Books).

Williamson, T. (1993), 'From interrogation to investigative interviewing: strategic trends in police questioning', *Journal of Community and Applied Social Psychology* vol. 3, pp. 89–99.

3

Helping the Police with their Enquiries outside the Police Station

Stephen Moston and Geoffrey M. Stephenson

In a study carried out post PACE, police officers indicated that when interviewing suspects their principal aim was most frequently to obtain a confession (Stephenson and Moston 1993). Not unnaturally, therefore, the right to silence has been an irritant of considerable proportions to police officers for many of whom a confession had become the key feature of the prosecution case. No wonder also that most officers attempt to break down a suspect's resolve to maintain silence, the two principal strategies employed being to persist with questioning, regardless, or to refer to the existence of other evidence which might persuade the suspect of the futility of remaining silent. More imaginatively, but more risky given the restrictions imposed by PACE, is to reason against the use of silence on the grounds that the benefits of cooperation outweigh those of resistance (Stephenson and Moston 1992). Moston and Stephenson (1993a) list in more detail the persuasive tactics now used by police officers to induce suspects to confess. These are distinctly less 'oppressive' than those detailed by Irving (1980) in a pre-PACE study, although in some few instances they contravene the spirit of the codes of practice and would, in the present climate of judicial practice, probably jeopardise acceptability to the court of any subsequent confession.

In the event, the number of suspects actually persuaded by police officers during interrogation to confess to the crime in question is small. When being tape-recorded, most suspects either confess early on in the absence of particular pressure to do so, or they consistently refuse to yield. Yet the number of suspects who confess does not seem to have changed greatly from what it was nigh on 20 years ago (Moston and Stephenson 1993a). It is against that

50

background that this chapter discusses the questioning and interviewing of suspects *outside* the police station and the recommendations put forward by the Royal Commission on Criminal Justice (1993) for changes to the regulations governing safeguards for the interviewing of suspects outside the police station. The discussion is based on the research study undertaken for the Royal Commission on Criminal Justice by Moston and Stephenson (1993b).

Existing constraints and practice

The Police and Criminal Evidence Act 1984 (PACE) and the codes of practice made under it introduced new rules governing the way in which suspects are arrested, detained and interviewed by police officers. The Act was intended to provide safeguards for both suspects and police officers. For example, Code C ensures that suspects are not subjected to undue pressure or oppression and makes it difficult for the police deliberately to record inaccurately or invent the words used by the suspect in response to questioning (Heaton-Armstrong 1989). On the other hand, the legislation was intended to make it difficult for a detained person to make unfounded allegations against the police, such as 'verballing', which might otherwise have appeared credible.

In their original form the codes of practice placed a number of controls on interviews inside the station, including tape recording, but were surprisingly vague about interviews conducted outside the police station. They rather gave the impression that interviews outside the station should not be taking place at all, but in the event that they did take place, it was not clear how far the restrictions placed on interviews inside the station should then apply. Some police officers who preferred to stick to the letter of the law, rather than its intention, found a number of loopholes which could be exploited (e.g., *R* v *Parchment* [1989] Crim LR 290; *R* v *Brezeanu* [1989] Crim LR 650). The problems concerning police malpractice in interviews therefore shifted away from the interview room to other locations, such as the police car *en route* to the station, where only contemporaneous notes (at best) could be kept (e.g., the case of *Hassan Khan*, cited in the *Independent*, 24 February 1990).

Concerns about interviews outside the police station were voiced in a number of reports. For example, Dixon et al. (1990, p. 133) argued that, '. . . there is the possibility that officers will try to evade recording and other controls by questioning suspects away from the interview room (at home during a post-arrest search, in the car on the way to the station, in the cell) or in the interview room before tape recording starts'. Similarly, Wolchover and Heaton-Armstrong (1991a) argued that since PACE came into effect, police officers 'have noticeably resorted to substantial questioning before arrival at the police station to an extent which used to be comparatively rare' (p. 242).

They suggest that such questioning is most likely to be reported when, perhaps following legal advice, suspects decline to make any comment inside the police station.

The shortcomings of the original codes of practice resulted in a series of three draft revisions, circulated between August 1989 and November 1990 (Wolchover and Heaton-Armstrong 1991a). The third and final draft was eventually accepted by Parliament in December 1990, becoming effective on 1 April 1991. The new codes included several revisions to the regulations concerning interviews with suspects outside the police station. Code C, para. 11.1, set out the following rules:

Following a decision to arrest a suspect he must not be interviewed about the relevant offence except at a police station (or other authorised place of detention) unless the consequent delay would be likely:

(a)   to lead to interference with or harm to evidence connected with an offence or interference with or physical harm to other persons; or

(b)   to lead to the alerting of other persons suspected of having committed an offence but not yet arrested for it; or

(c)   to hinder the recovery of property obtained in consequence of the commission of an offence.

Interviewing in any of these circumstances should cease once the relevant risk has been averted or the necessary questions have been put in order to attempt to avert that risk.

The revised codes also make it clear that every interview that takes place must be recorded (Code C, para. 11.5), regardless of where the interview took place. Under Code C, para. 11.13, officers are now also obliged to record any comments made by the suspected person, including unsolicited remarks, which are outside the context of an interview but which might be relevant to the offence.

Note for guidance 11A in Code C offers a further clarification of the law, making a clear distinction between what are regarded as the separate activities of questioning and interviewing:

An interview is the questioning of a person regarding his involvement or suspected involvement in a criminal offence or offences. Questioning a person only to obtain information or his explanation of the facts or in the ordinary course of the officer's duties does not constitute an interview for the purpose of this code. Neither does questioning which is confined to the proper and effective conduct of a search.

In the codes, therefore, the procedure of *questioning* a potential suspect is viewed as being quite distinct from *interviewing*. A key consequence of the difference between these two forms of encounter with suspects is that interviews must be recorded, whereas there are no such controls on questioning. However, if a suspect should make an admission or other form of damaging statement in response to questioning then the officer concerned should make a record of that statement and caution the suspect.

The revised codes of practice have not been an unqualified success in redefining interviews outside the police station. Several commentators have raised doubts as to how effective the codes would be in practice. Wolchover and Heaton-Armstrong (1991a) suggested that the ban on interviews between the decision to arrest and arrival at the police station sounded 'the death-knell' for most 'car-seat' interviews, although they anticipated that officers would try to stretch the definitions of exceptional circumstances, with 'imaginative officers dreaming up all manner of ingenious pretexts' (p. 243). More likely, attempting to regulate police conduct outside the station by formally categorising police enquiries of suspects and potential suspects is a doomed exercise. This is because the formal distinction between 'interviewing' and 'questioning' is difficult to sustain in practice, and because there will be many times when officers outside the station feel compelled by the demands of the situation to continue what is proving to be a fruitful line of questioning, regardless of the rule book. Such behaviour is not necessarily mischievous, as is implied by some commentators, and may in any case be justified if needs be by reference to the exceptional circumstances listed above.

We have investigated the conversations that officers actually report having with suspects outside the station, and we have also examined some of the consequences of these conversations following arrest. Our discussion will be organised around three recommendations (numbers 38–40) proposed by the Royal Commission and we shall discuss the rationale for these proposals. The data cited in this paper are derived from a questionnaire-based study carried out in three police forces (Bedfordshire, Cumbria and the Metropolitan Police) featuring a total of 641 suspects for whom custody records were issued (for full details on the methodology of this study and the cases featured see Moston and Stephenson 1993b). We begin by outlining the incidence of questioning and interviewing and other conversations outside the police station and we then address the Royal Commission's recommendations.

Questioning of suspects outside the police station

Of the 641 suspects in the survey, 201 (31%) were reportedly questioned prior to their arrest. In 154 (77%) cases in which suspects were questioned the stated purpose was to establish whether or not a crime had been committed. The other main reason given was to eliminate the suspect from enquiries (42 cases, 21%). In five cases (2%) the suspect was initially thought to be merely a potential eyewitness.

Most questioning prior to arrest took place at crime scenes (61% of the 201 cases) or at the home of the suspect (about 19% of the 201 cases). About 12% of suspects were questioned inside the police station. Questioning inside police cars was reported very rarely (only two cases).

There was a considerable degree of variation in the amount of questioning carried out in each of the three forces. The levels of questioning ranged from a low of 21% in Bedfordshire, 28% in Cumbria to a high of 52% in the Metropolitan stations.

Caucasian and Asian suspects were less likely to be questioned prior to arrest than Afro-Caribbean suspects. The difference was consistent for all three police forces and in all of the offences where the numbers were sufficient for comparison.

Interviewing of suspects outside the police station

A total of 52 of the 641 suspects (8.1%) were reported to have been *interviewed* prior to arrival at the police station. Thirty of these suspects (57.7%) had been questioned prior to the interview. In 20 of the 52 cases (38.5%) the interview was initiated by a police officer, in 29 cases (55.8%) the suspect was said to have initiated the interview and in three cases (5.8%) the interview was seen as being initiated by another person, that is, the statement of a third party, such as a store detective, prompted the police officer or suspect to say something which then initiated an interview.

Interviews took place primarily at the crime scene or in a police car on the way to the station. Six of the interviews conducted 'outside the police station' were in fact, conducted inside the station but outside the interview room. In one case the interview took place in the private car of an off-duty officer who had witnessed an accident involving a stolen car.

Table 3.1 The reasons given for interviews (outside the police station)

Reason for interview	Number of cases	Percentage of cases
Establish involvement in crime	12	23.1
Establish if crime committed	7	13.5
To gather evidence	11	21.2
To identify other suspects	1	1.9
Suspect asked what would happen	6	11.5
Statement of suspect	14	26.9
Development of conversation	1	1.9

Officers cited a number of reasons why interviews had taken place (see table 3.1). In 23% of cases officers gave as the reason 'to establish the person's involvement in an offence'. This is in accordance with the notes for guidance in Code C. In one case an interview was conducted to identify other suspects. One of the reasons cited (to identify whether or not a crime had occurred) is properly covered under the definition of questioning rather than interviewing. The reason 'to gather evidence' is very imprecise. In a number of cases it was allegedly the suspect who initiated the interview, either by asking what would happen to them, or by making some other statement. The one case in which an interview developed out of a non-offence-related conversation occurred when a suspect arrested in another force was being driven to one of the forces in the study.

Non-offence-related conversations outside the police station

We felt it was implausible that police officers, having decided to caution a suspect, would henceforth cease all communication with the suspect. We therefore included questions about the extent to which 'non-offence-related conversations' took place.

Officers reported having had 'extensive' conversations with suspects in 43 cases (5.5%), and limited conversations in 163 cases (25.4%). Conversations that were restricted to the minimum necessary for politeness occurred in 223 cases (34.8%) and in 220 cases (34.3%) officers reported having had no non-offence-related conversations whatsoever. These figures are of interest, if only for the fact that police officers often claim to make what are colloquially called 'deaf and dumb' arrests, in which arrest and caution are said to take place without eliciting a reply from the suspect, with 'no other conversation' taking place. This appears to be merely a convenient fiction, at least in a significant proportion of cases.

In the questionnaire the officers were asked whether or not any of these non-offence-related conversations had been tape-recorded. The results showed that in 42 cases (6.6%) tape recorders were used.

Character of interviews outside the police station

Let us exmaine in detail the 52 cases in which suspects were interviewed outside the police station, looking specifically at the evidence obtained.

Table 3.2 Outcomes of interviews outside the police station

Outcome of interview	Number of cases	Percentage of cases
Full confession (facts and intent)	21	40.4
Admit facts, denial of intent	8	15.4
Other damaging admission	9	17.3
Said nothing at all	0	0.0
Denied that offence occurred	5	9.6
Denial, no alibi	2	3.8
Denial, with alibi	4	7.7
Other offences	2	3.8
Missing	1	1.9
Total	52	99.9

Table 3.2 shows the outcomes of the 52 interviews conducted outside the police station. In one case data were missing.

There was a high number of confessions and admissions amongst the sample of 52 cases, with nearly three quarters of suspects making some form of admission. This rate is higher than the rate of admissions obtained when interviews take place inside the police station where confessions and admissions occur in only about 59% of cases. Although no suspects said nothing at all, four of the 52 suspects (7.7%) — each of whom denied the allegations against them — used their right of silence during these interviews. In two cases the outcome of the interview was ambiguously recorded as 'other offences'.

The high confession/admission rate during interviews conducted outside the station can be explained by making reference to the reasons why interviews took place. Apart from the cases in which an interview was conducted when questioning would have been more appropriate, there are three main reasons for interviews outside the station, which have a bearing on the high confession rate, as follows:

(a) Some interviews appear to have been initiated by the suspect, although one cannot be certain that there were no prior exchanges with the police. These suspects may be more likely than other suspects to make spontaneous confessions. The sample of suspects interviewed outside the police station is therefore not truly representative, to the extent that it is a self-selecting group.

(b) Another reason for the initiation of interviews is a question from the suspect, who asks what is going to happen. In Irving's (1980) research such a request was seen as a willingness on the part of the suspect to enter into negotiations (or bargaining) over the content of a future statement and the likely outcome of detention. For example, a suspect might state, 'I'll admit it if I can have bail'. The officer's response to this request for information may have a bearing on the outcome of any subsequent interview.

(c) Some interviews are carried out to 'gather evidence'. These may be either important cases or simply those in which officers want to obtain an early admission. The ambiguous nature of the explanation 'to gather evidence' makes it difficult to clarify why officers deemed an interview to be necessary, but it does seem likely that in many of these cases police officers are specifically seeking confessions at the time of arrest.

Although it is clear from the PACE codes of practice that all interviews should be recorded, a surprisingly high number of the 52 interviews outside the station (32 cases, or 61.5%) were not contemporaneously recorded. In only one case (1.9%) was the record made on a designated form for contemporaneous notes, whilst in the other 19 cases (36.5%), records were made in officers' pocketbooks. In some of the 32 cases of unrecorded interviews it is possible that records were made after arrival at the police station.

In 15 of the 20 cases when records were made prior to arrival at the police station, suspects were given a chance to check the record (prior to arrival at the station) and of these 15 cases the record was signed in 11 cases. Six of the interviews were tape-recorded, although this fact did not seem to form part of the official record of the interview. In summary, of the 52 interviews, records were ostensibly kept, checked and then signed prior to arrival at the police station in only 11 cases. These results were not exclusively associated with any one police force. It should also be noted that the outcome of interviews was not related to who initiated the interview. There is a high number of admissions regardless of who opened the interview.

Outcomes of interviews conducted outside and inside the police station

Interviews conducted outside the designated interviewing room are for the most part not recorded, and are no doubt frequently entered into by suspects who have not considered at length the wisdom of so doing. It goes without saying that solicitors or their representatives are unlikely to be present at interviews outside the station, a factor which in itself reduces the possibility that the right to silence will be exercised. It is, therefore, of considerable interest to ask if the occurrence of interviews outside the station is directly related to the outcome of interviews inside the station. Will interviews outside the station prejudice the decision to exercise the right to silence in the more formal setting of the police station?

Table 3.3 Interviews outside the police station and the outcome of interviews inside the police station

	Number and percentage of outcomes of interviews inside the police station		
	Admission	*Said nothing*	*Denial*
No interviews outside station	292 (56.8%)	29 (5.6%)	193 (37.5%)
Interviewed outside station	36 (81.8%)	3 (6.8%)	5 (11.4%)

The study did, indeed, find a link between interviews conducted outside the police station and the outcome of those conducted inside the station, which is shown in table 3.3. Outcomes of interviews inside the station have been collapsed into three categories, confessions/admissions, saying nothing, and denials. Suspects who had been interviewed outside the station were highly likely to make admissions in the station and far less likely to deny an accusation. Only 18% of those who are interviewed outside the station fail to admit their guilt inside the station. The correspoonding figure for those who are not interviewed outside is 43%. At least from the police perspective the case for carrying out such interviews seems very strong indeed.

Table 3.4 Non-offence-related conversations outside the police station and the outcome of interviews inside the police station

Extent of non-offence-related conversation outside police station	*Number and percentage of outcomes of interviews inside the police station*		
	Admission	*Said nothing*	*Denial*
No conversation	91 (47.9%)	14 (7.4%)	85 (44.7%)
Minimum conversation	123 (61.8%)	12 (6.0%)	64 (32.2%)
Limited conversation	92 (63.9%)	6 (4.2%)	46 (31.9%)
Extensive conversation	23 (82.1%)	1 (3.6%)	4 (14.3%)

Of equal, if not greater interest, is the question of a possible link between 'non-offence-related conversations' held outside the station, and behaviour within the interviewing room. On the face of it, officers should not be more inclined to strike up friendly conversations with the guilty than the not guilty, or with those who subsequently admit rather than with those who deny the offences. That is, however, exactly what seemed to happen in practice. There was a strong link between the extent of non-offence-related conversations held on the way to the police station and the outcome of subsequent tape-recorded interviews. Table 3.4 shows that the more extensive the non-offence-related conversations the higher the number of subsequent admissions.

There are a number of possible explanations for this result, centering on who initiated the conversation. It may be that some suspects are, for reasons of personality, more likely to 'chat' with police officers. These 'friendly' suspects may be more inclined to make admissions because they want to please the interviewing officer, raising concerns over certain forms of false confession (see Gudjonsson and MacKeith 1988). Another possibility is that something said by officers during non-offence-related conversations may be having an effect on subsequent interviews. For example, officers may make comments about the possibility of bail or offer other inducements. A less worrying possibility might simply be that officers use the time prior to arrival at the police station to engage in 'rapport building' and that they are especially likely to attempt this with suspects against whom the evidence seems strongest. Rapport building is often advocated on police interview training courses as a means of gaining the cooperation of a suspect, but it is very rare to find evidence of any such conversations appearing on taped interviews (see Moston and Engelberg 1993). It is of interest to note that there is virtually no difference between those who inside the station 'said nothing' and those who 'denied' the offence in their tendency either to have been interviewed outside the station or to have held non-offence-related conversations. This does rather suggest that the conversational initiative has generally been taken by the officer rather than the suspect, in that those intent on silence would be more likely to hold their tongues than those intent on denial. Whichever of these or other possible hypotheses applies, the inadequacy of tape recording inside the police station as a wholly accurate record of all relevant verbal exchanges between suspect and interviewer is apparent.

Questioning as defined by Code C need not be recorded, and we have seen that questioning was frequently reported in our sample of cases. However, unlike reported interviews and non-offence-related conversations, questioning was not independently related to the outcomes of interviews inside the station. Questioning is probably a more routine matter than is interviewing, and does not seem to have the longer-term significance of either the interview or supposedly non-offence-related conversation. Finally, it should be noted that there were no links between any form of encounter outside the police station and the decision to take legal advice.

Degree of correspondence between evidence obtained through interviews outside the police station and evidence obtained inside the police station

There was a high degree of correspondence between statements made outside the station and those made inside the station. Of the 44 suspects whom the police say were interviewed outside as well as inside the station, 35 gave

59

consistent replies. That is, initial admissions or denials were repeated inside the station. Of the remaining suspects, five who had initially denied having committed an offence changed their responses towards admissions. Three suspects who had initially made an admission subsequently declined to say anything about the offence (using their right to silence) and one suspect changed from an admission to a denial.

In 19 cases in which suspects had been interviewed outside the police station, tapes of the subsequent interviews inside the police station were collected. It had initially been intended that an analysis of the content of these two sources of information would be examined to determine how the officer, or the suspect, made links between the two interviews. However, in only five of the taped interviews was there any direct reference to the existence of the earlier interview. This is somewhat surprising. One might have expected that the earlier statement of the suspect would form an integral part of the taped interview, but this is simply not the case. In the majority of cases an independent observer would not realise that an earlier interview had taken place.

In the five cases in the current sample in which reference was made to earlier interviews, on three occasions it was the interviewing officer who brought up the subject, each time to prompt the suspect to restate an earlier incriminating statement; for example, 'You had said there was someone else involved'. In another case the suspect was asked why he was prepared to implicate a friend inside the station, when he had earlier claimed to be working alone. The suspect replied as follows, 'I was in the back of your car. I was full of nerves. I've never been in the back of a police car before.' Replies such as this may partially explain why officers are reluctant to raise the topic of interviews outside the station. If the suspect disagrees with any aspect of the earlier statement the reason for this alteration needs to be defined. Suspects are likely either to suggest that they were nervous or confused, or in the worst scenario for the police officer, to suggest that the admission had been coerced. In either situation the validity of the earlier statement is called into question.

Recommendations of the Royal Commission

The results we have described have a bearing on three recommendations by the Royal Commission on Criminal Justice (1993) concerning the safeguards for interviewing outside the police stations. These are as follows.

Recommendation 38. The definition of an interview in Code C note for guidance 11A should be clarified to remove the apparent confusion as to what constitutes an interview.

Recommendation 39. If the tape recording of exchanges between officers and suspects outside the police station proves feasible, the PACE codes should be extended to cover what is permissible between arrest outside the station and arrival in it.

Recommendation 40. Confessions outside the police station should be put to the suspect at the beginning of a tape-recorded interview.

The revised codes of practice have sought to eliminate interviews outside the police station, except in certain specified circumstances, thereby in theory enhancing the importance of questioning. However, officers are also aware that it is difficult to make sharp distinctions between questioning and interviewing, and given the concerns over interviews outside the police station, they may err on the side of caution by waiting until they have the use of a tape recorder inside the police station before commencing any form of dialogue. This could lead to a number of problems, such as a waste of resources, in that a greater number of suspects are likely to be arrested and then interviewed inside the police station than is strictly necessary. Current training initiatives are trying to offer clarification for officers over the circumstances in which there is a need for them to conduct questioning, and this aspect of training may need further elaboration.

This confusion between interviewing and questioning is recognised by recommendation 38. However, no solution to the confusion is proposed, and clarification is likely to prove a difficult process. Even if new definitions are achieved, training officers to make the necessary distinctions will prove cumbersome.

The current ambiguities between questioning and interviewing experienced by police officers seem certain to result in a number of legal disputes. For example, an appeal in one case, *R* v *Cox* (1992) 96 Cr App R 464 centred on the admissibility of statements made by the suspect in response to questioning. The appeal court ruled that the questions did in fact constitute an interview, since their purpose was to elicit an admission. One important aspect of this case was that the ambiguities in the wording of the codes of practice were acknowledged. For example, the Court of Appeal referred to the 'difficulty of grasping the meaning' of note 11A, and that if applied literally, a number of confusions might arise since the purpose of many interviews was to obtain information from a suspect or to obtain that person's explanation of the facts.

With respect to recommendation 39, the current study has shown that some officers are already carrying personal tape recorders and it is anticipated that pilot studies on the feasibility of carrying personal tape recorders will, indeed, prove successful. The figures given here concerning the incidence of use of such tape recorders (about 6%) are probably a conservative estimate. Other officers may well be carrying tape recorders, but are reluctant to admit that they are doing so. This may be either because they fear disciplinary action, or merely because they do not view the tapes as being officially relevant. The fact that some officers do already carry tape recorders, no doubt encouraged by articles such as those in *Police Review* by Heaton-Armstrong and Wolchover (1991b), suggests that, should portable tape recorders be issued, then simple arguments against their use, such as 'they weigh too much', should not be given a great deal of consideration.

However, the arguments in favour of portable tape recorders are complex. The use of portable tape recorders would undoubtedly improve the quality of information gathered at the time of arrest and prior to arrival at the police station. Its most important effect would be to improve the quality and validity of interviews inside the police station, which would no longer be conducted unrealistically as if they represented the totality of the understanding achieved between police and suspect.

One additional advantage, at least to the police, of the regular use of tape recorders to record all exchanges with the suspect (as well as witnesses) is that it would remove some of the current stigma concerning exchanges outside the police station. The current study clearly shows that discussions (i.e., interviewing and other conversations) between the suspect and the arresting officer have a bearing on the outcome of tape-recorded interviews. It therefore cannot be argued convincingly that the use of tape or even video recording inside the station presents a full picture of police interviewing practices. The taped interview represents only a partial picture of a suspect's exchanges with police officers and may in many cases be a stage-managed and sanitised version of police interviewing procedures taken as a whole.

The key advantage in the provision of portable tape recorders would be to compel recognition of the existence and importance of exchanges outside the interview room. Discussing the topic of interviews outside the police station sometimes has a surreal flavour, with some officers living under the pretence that they do not occur. Recommendation 40 (and also see recommendation 87) goes some way towards officially recognising interviews outside the station in that confessions would be restated at the start of the first interview inside the police station. In a small number of cases suspects do appear to change their statements between interviews, although in the majority of cases suspects make consistent statements. This proposal is nonetheless problematic in that its emphasis is clearly on bolstering evidence against the suspect, the information from interviews apparently being relevant only if it implicates the suspect. This is anomalous because it effectively conspires to conceal denials and explanations made by the suspect outside the station. And, of course, questioning and other non-offence-related conversations would not be covered by this proposal.

The provision of portable tape recorders would not automatically mean an end to arguments over police interviewing practices. There will always be scope for officers to have a quiet word 'off the record' and, similarly, for a suspect to argue that the tape recorder was not turned on until after a 'discussion'. In reality, there is simply no practicable way to record or monitor every possible occasion in which a police officer has an opportunity to speak with a suspect, nor should such a demeaning practice be necessary in a properly recruited and trained profession. Nonetheless, using available recording techniques in all reasonable circumstances can only enhance responsible and effective investigative interviewing.

Portable tape recorders may also become an important tool in the investigative process for the questioning of witnesses. This seems a sensible step forward, since it too would help to remove the current overemphasis on interviews with the suspect inside the police station, by providing alternative and valuable information at a time when witnesses have the events clearly in mind. Witnesses' recorded statements might subsequently be used to check hypotheses, clarify error and suggest new lines of enquiry. For example, innocent persons may become suspects in investigations following a misleading interview with a witness, and the existence of taped records of interviews with witnesses might subsequently clarify how an investigation became sidetracked.

The potential forensic value of interviews conducted outside the station — with both witnesses and suspects — will no doubt be enhanced by the use of tape recording, as will the ability of the courts to evaluate the worth of confessions made at the police station. The dangers stem from the fact that tape recording will convey a respectability to interviews outside the station, and that they will come to be favoured by police officers as a more effective means of obtaining confession evidence than are interviews conducted in the comparative calm and formality of the police station. It will not be feasible outside to provide the additional safeguards and protection of rights — including that of silence — currently afforded at the station.

As will have become clear by now, the current codes of practice are unclear about the regulation of police conversations with suspects outside the police station and it is obviously the case that what is to be permitted should be clarified. One obvious omission from the current codes of practice is the requirement for officers to state in the record of interview why the interview took place. In the majority of cases in this study the rationale for interviewing is obscure (e.g., 'to gather evidence'). In the absence of any requirement to justify an interview at the time that it occurs, there is considerable scope for interviewers to devise *post hoc* explanations that meet the criteria set out in the codes of practice. Also missing from the current legislation is any requirement for officers to explain why, following questioning, a person is subsequently arrested. Presumably the questioned person says something that precipitates the arrest, but this information is unlikely to be recorded in detail. The legislation covers incriminating statements only. The introduction of portable tape recorders will merely increase the urgency with which the codes of practice should be expanded to deal with these and other anomalies in the protection of suspects' rights outside the station.

Conclusion

In a large number of cases suspects are questioned, interviewed or have other conversations with police officers prior to their arrival at the police station. In most cases there is no record of the content of these exchanges. Even when records are ostensibly kept, they are typically inadequate. Even under ideal circumstances, contemporaneous notes are not suited for encounters outside the police station and there are strong arguments in favour of the provision of portable tape recorders. The recommendations by the Royal Commission are largely to be welcomed although they are for the most part merely defining problems, not providing solutions. The dispute over the distinction between interviewing and questioning itself looks set to continue for the foreseeable future. However, it should be noted that one aim of the codes of practice was to curtail interviews outside the police station. The reportedly small number of such interviews may seem to suggest that the aim was achieved. Our results indicate, however, that totally unrecorded but relevant conversations were conducted on a wide scale, and that a knowledge of the content of these conversations is required to ensure that the court has a good understanding of the context in which tape-recorded interviews are conducted inside the station.

References

Dixon, D., Bottomley, K., Cole, C., Gill, M., and Wall, D. (1990), 'Safeguarding the rights of suspects in police custody', *Policing and Society*, vol. 1, pp. 115-40.

Gudjonsson, G.H., and MacKeith, J.A.C. (1988), 'Retracted confessions: Legal, psychological and psychiatric aspects', *Medicine, Science and the Law*, vol. 28, pp. 187-94.

Heaton-Armstrong, A. (1989), 'An end to verbals', *Police Review*, vol. 7, pp. 1376-7.

Irving, B. (1980), *Police Interrogation: A Case Study of Current Practice* (Royal Commission on Criminal Procedure Research Study No. 2) (London: HMSO).

Moston, S., and Engelberg, T. (1993), 'Police questioning techniques in tape-recorded interviews with criminal suspects', to appear in *Policing and Society*.

Moston, S.J., and Stephenson, G.M. (1993a), 'The changing face of police interrogation', *Journal of Community and Applied Social Psychology*, vol. 3, pp. 101–15.

Moston, S.J., and Stephenson, G.M. (1993b), *The Questioning and Interviewing of Suspects outside the Police Station* (Royal Commission on Criminal Justice Research Study No. 22) (London: HMSO).

Royal Commission on Criminal Justice (1993), *Report* (Cm 2263) (London: HMSO).

Stephenson, G.M., and Moston, S.J. (1992), 'The effect of the right to silence on the prosecution and conviction of criminal suspects', in F. Lösel, D. Bender and T. Bliesner (eds), *Psychology of Law: International Perspectives* (Berlin: de Gruyter).

Stephenson, G.M., and Moston S.J. (1993), 'Attitudes and assumptions of police officers when questioning criminal suspects', in *Issues in Criminological and Legal Psychology*, No. 18 (Leicester: British Psychological Society), pp. 30-6.

Wolchover, D., and Heaton-Armstrong, A. (1991a), 'The questioning code revamped', *Criminal Law Review*, pp. 232-51.

Wolchover, D., and Heaton-Armstrong, A., (1991b), 'Cracking the codes', *Police Review* (12 April), pp. 751-3.

4

Police Interrogation: What Are the Rules of the Game?

John Baldwin

The background

The interviewing of suspects is regarded by most informed observers as a critical — perhaps the most critical — stage in the processing of almost all criminal cases. Police investigators see such interviews in the same light themselves, and there are very few criminal cases indeed of any seriousness in which the suspect is not interrogated by police officers. It is almost a truism to observe also that the outcome of the interview with a suspect tends to colour decisions that are subsequently made when the case is processed by the police and the prosecuting authorities (see, for instance, McConville and Baldwin 1982).

Despite the importance attached to interrogation, it has only been in the recent past that anything of significance has been discovered about what happens behind the closed doors of the police interview room. A good deal of research, discussed by Gudjonsson 1992 and by Moston et al. 1992, has been conducted into the characteristics of those who confess and into the significance of confessions in the criminal process, but there have been few forays into the interview room itself. A major impediment to such study in the past has been a reluctance on the part of the police service at all levels to allow researchers (or anyone else for that matter) access to the interview room. However, with the introduction of recording machinery in police stations in recent years, the interview room has become much more accessible to outside scrutiny.

Deficiencies in interviews

The present writer has been carrying out research on police interview procedures for several years (including projects for the Royal Commission on

Criminal Justice: see Baldwin 1992a) and has in the process played many hundreds of tapes of interview (see Baldwin 1992b; 1993a). The research has been mainly conducted in the West Midlands, West Mercia and the Metropolitan Police District. The standards of police interviewing as they have been assessed in this research have been very variable, and it has become apparent that the quality of much police interviewing is very poor.[1]

The present writer experienced no great difficulty in identifying a number of basic deficiencies in police interviewing (Baldwin 1993a). It emerged, for instance, that many interviews are ill-planned; procedures are often inadequately explained to suspects;[2] and officers are in many cases hell-bent on securing a confession, operating on the basis of a strong presumption of guilt from the outset. In some cases, officers adopt harrying and confrontational tactics in interviews.

It is, however, surprising that the single most striking characteristic of police interviewing to emerge from the author's examination of the tapes of interview is its general ineptitude. Much interviewing is simply feeble and aimless, scarcely matching the macho image of police interviewers as professional, skilled and forceful interrogators. The tapes reveal instead that many officers are nervous, ill at ease and evidently lacking in confidence. Even in the simplest cases, officers can be seen with their eyes glued to a written statement which they have evidently not even bothered to read before embarking on the interview.

It also clearly emerged that police training can be regarded as no panacea, and no matter how carefully training courses are devised, they can do no more than ameliorate the situation. Indeed, in this writer's view, it is often the officers who have received most training in interviewing who turn out to be the least

---

[1] The assessment of standards of interviewing is problematic. The meaning to be attached to the processes of detention and questioning is complex, and the tapes of interview can offer only limited insights into the social context (or the 'social construction') of interrogation. What constitutes a 'good' or an 'effective' interview is largely a subjective judgment, and questioning that, say, a psychologist would regard as overbearing or coercive might well be seen very differently by police officers, civil libertarians or indeed suspects. Making assessments of standards of interviewing, therefore, represents a minefield for the academic researcher, and the best that the present writer could do was to seek to apply to the interviews on tape the standards of good interviewing practice adopted in other situations. These standards were taken to include the following: allowing suspects an unhurried and uninterrupted opportunity to state their position; listening to their responses; avoiding harrying, coercive or authoritarian tactics; and testing a suspect's account with fairness and integrity. For further discussion of the difficulties encountered in making these assessments and the criteria that were employed in this study, see Baldwin 1993a, pp. 328–9.

[2] This is very evident in relation to the administering of the police caution. In over a tenth of the cases observed, and as many as a third in one of the stations examined, the caution was delivered to suspects in such a garbled manner as to be virtually incomprehensible. Sometimes it was not given at all. The preliminary explanation of the procedures to be followed in the interview was also frequently inadequate.

competent interviewers and vice versa (Baldwin 1992b, pp. 9–12). It needs to be recognised and accepted that there will remain a hard core of officers who, whatever training they are given, cannot safely be left to interview suspects on their own.

Given the nature of these difficulties, it might have been anticipated that the recommendations of the Royal Commission on Criminal Justice would go some way to improving matters. Police interviewing procedures were central to the Commission's concerns and assume a prominent place in its lengthy report (1993, ch. 3). In the writer's view, however, it is unlikely that these recommendations will in practice make much difference to current interviewing standards.

The basic problem with the Royal Commission's recommendations, insofar as they impinged upon the police station, was that they were consolidatory rather than innovatory in character (Baldwin 1993b). No fundamental rethinking of existing procedures was apparently deemed necessary or desirable. The report contained, for example, certain proposals designed to bolster the tape recording of interviews so that more of the informal discussions that take place with suspects get recorded; recommendations intended to strengthen the position of custody officers, and measures which sought to facilitate suspects' access to legal advice. These are worthy enough objectives, but many of the changes that were proposed were minor in character, much existing practice was left untouched, and some of the really awkward questions were not confronted at all.

It is true that there were some useful measures in the package put forward by the Commission relating to suspects' rights in police custody, for example, the recommendation that there be continuous video monitoring of custody areas and adjacent passages (Royal Commission on Criminal Justice 1993, para. 36). In the main, however, one was struck by the bland, unexceptionable and unimaginative character of the Commission's recommendations on police interview procedures. There was a pervasive air of superficiality in the discussion, a superficiality that was compounded by an almost complete neglect of the small mountain of research evidence on the detention and questioning of suspects, assembled in the post-PACE era. There was little more than a respectful nod in the direction of this body of research, and the focus was instead upon the Commission's own research studies as if these had been conducted in a vacuum.

In its report, the Royal Commission commended the progress that has been made in the past year by the police and the Law Society in seeking to overcome the difficulties. In the case of the police, the Central Planning and Training Unit produced early in 1993 two manuals for police interviewers — a 35-page booklet, *A Guide to Interviewing*, and a 57-page booklet, *The Interviewer's*

Rule Book — which have been distributed to all police interviewers throughout the country.[3] The Commission also advocates that the Law Society's booklet, *Advising a Suspect in the Police Station*, now in its 3rd edition, which sets out guidance on the solicitor's role at the police station, be 'more widely known, better understood, and more consistently acted upon' (Royal Commission on Criminal Justice 1993, para. 60).[4]

While the Commission's commendation of these moves may well be sensible, it is very unlikely that many police interviewers will trouble to study the Law Society's materials or that many legal advisers will read the police documents. The basic problem with such guidance has always been that it is not widely read even by those for whom it is intended, let alone by the other parties involved in interviews. Furthermore, the materials themselves have no status in law, so that even if the relevant documents were to be read, there is no guarantee whatever that their validity would be accepted.[5] In other words, although the police service and the Law Society are striving to offer advice and guidance to their own members, it cannot be assumed that this will be accepted as authoritative by other parties involved in interviews. There is no consensus (nor, as far as one can tell, much dialogue) between the police service and the Law Society on such matters.

The ground rules

The fundamental difficulty in bringing about such a consensus is that there is little common ground between the Law Society and the police service on what should be the basic rules to be followed by the participants in police interviews. In such a difficult and contentious area, where mutual suspicion and mistrust run deep, it is less than half the battle to educate one of the parties. The difficulty is two-sided, and police interviewers are in just as much need of clarification

---

[3] A marked shift in emphasis in police interviewing is advocated in these manuals. Robust and manipulative techniques are jettisoned in favour of much more subtle approaches. The stated objective is 'to discover the truth about the matter under investigation, to gather information and to obtain evidence'. Interviewers are urged to be 'polite at all times', and common courtesy is seen as being a more effective approach than confrontation.

[4] It is possible to discern a markedly tougher and more strident character to the guidance offered to solicitors in each successive edition of the Law Society's handbook. In the past year, the Law Society has not only produced a new training kit for legal advisers but has also introduced a number of courses on a nationwide basis on police station advice. The Legal Aid Board's stated intention to introduce rigorous accreditation standards (which will mean in practice that only 'accredited' legal advisers will qualify for payment under the legal aid scheme) is also likely to improve matters.

[5] Considerable controversy was generated a few years ago when police interviewers in some parts of the country were accused by solicitors of cynically misleading suspects by quoting passages from the Law Society's handbook out of context, in order to persuade them to ignore advice given to them by their own legal adviser.

of the rules that apply (and in particular those relating to the lawyer's role at interviews) as are the lawyers.[6]

Given the intractable nature of these problems, the Royal Commission's hope that a solution might be found in a rewording of certain paragraphs in the relevant code of practice and in police training (which should, it is argued, 'include formal instruction in the role that solicitors are properly expected to play in the criminal justice system including the reasons why they should, from time to time, protect their clients in a way which the police may see as unhelpful': Royal Commission on Criminal Justice 1993, para. 54) is unlikely to prove much more than wishful thinking. It is disappointing that, in an area where so many antagonisms and conflicting perceptions are held by different groups, the Royal Commission did not itself seize the opportunity to settle some of these issues one way or another.[7]

In the light of the conflicts and uncertainties that continue to dog police interviewing, the guidance offered by the professional bodies cannot be more than partial or provide answers to the many dilemmas and questions that confront the parties daily. There is, for example, no firm rule on whether police interviewers are permitted to shout or swear at suspects.[8] Nor is it established whether they are justified in lying, or misleading a suspect, as to the strength of the available evidence. It is not decided how much pressure can legitimately be exerted upon an individual who wishes to remain silent, or how long an interview can proceed in the face of a suspect's silence. Officers have at present no firm guidance on whether they can relentlessly fire questions at a silent suspect without the interview becoming oppressive within the meaning of s. 76 of PACE. And when a legal adviser does intervene to object to the way an interview is being conducted, no one can say for certain whether the interviewer is at liberty simply to ignore the objection.[9]

---

[6] The points made about the lawyer's role in police interviews might also be made about that played by appropriate adults.

[7] The conflicting perceptions of the parties are well illustrated in the new guidance that has been issued to the police. Though a much less confrontational approach towards suspects is now being advocated than in earlier years, the new techniques will make life tricky for legal advisers, since the boundaries between propriety and impropriety in police questioning will become ever more difficult to define. The use of silence as a technique employed to put pressure on suspects is one example of the difficulties that advisers will face. It is not obvious that the Royal Commission recognised such difficulties.

[8] It has only been in extreme cases that the Court of Appeal has taken such strong objection to particular interrogation tactics that it has said that an interview is 'oppressive' within the meaning of PACE, s. 76. In the recent example of the Cardiff Three (*R* v *Paris* (1993) 97 Cr App R 99), the Court of Appeal expressed itself 'horrified' at the way that Miller was bullied and hectored in some parts of a long series of interviews. In those interviews with Miller (a man on the boundary of mental handicap), the court said that it was 'undoubtedly oppressive ... to shout at a suspect ... what they wanted him to say after he had denied involvement over 300 times'.

[9] On one tape examined by the writer, a legal adviser was told to 'shut up' by one of the police interviewers when she tried to intervene. It is difficult to know what a competent legal adviser is entitled to do even in this extreme situation.

As far as police interviewing practice is concerned, the most pressing issues now to be determined relate not to machinery or procedures but to questions of principle and prevailing attitudes — attitudes which in the past have been affected to only a limited extent by rule changes, exhortations, training or supervisory procedures (see the provocative discussion by McConville et al. (1991, ch. 10)). Such attitudes are to a considerable extent the product of police culture and folklore, and as such are extremely difficult to shift. The Royal Commission's blandishments to the police and to other groups seem in consequence unlikely to produce any major change in attitudes if recent history provides a guide.

Many of the problems that confront the participants in police interviews remain unresolved (and at present are unresolvable) because there is no consensus amongst the conflicting interests about the object of the exercise. The legal and procedural rules that exist to regulate the conduct of interviews are extremely vague and uncertain. Very little guidance is offered, for example, in the relevant legislation or the accompanying codes of practice. And the Court of Appeal has itself had little to say about what kind of questioning is fair and permissible and what will be regarded as 'oppressive'.[10]

The Royal Commission had little to say about the vagueness of the guidance available to interviewers. It saw the solution to the current difficulties in training, supervision and the monitoring of performance by 'occasional empirical research'. The problems are, however, too deep-rooted and endemic to be solved as easily as this implies. The main problem is to determine what kind of pressures police interviewers can legitimately exert upon suspects detained in police custody. Without some resolution of this central issue, training is likely to be ineffective, if not misguided.

It is not surprising, therefore, that cases continue to arise in which there are genuine disputes between the parties on these matters.[11] One might have thought that the recording of interviews would have provided enough raw material from which a moderately imaginative defence lawyer might launch an effective challenge to the way an interview has been conducted. But challenges

---

[10]The Court of Appeal has resolved a great many cases arising from the conduct of police interrogation procedures in the post-PACE period. Few of these cases, however, have raised issues which are directly relevant to the conduct of interviews themselves. The principal issues on which the court has focused in these cases have been the denial of access to a legal adviser and the definition of what constitutes an 'interview'. See generally the discussion in Feldman 1990.

[11]A striking illustration of this arose in the recent acquittal of George Heron in a murder trial in Northumberland following the ruling by the trial judge that the police interview was oppressive. The police and Crown Prosecution Service were reported as genuinely astonished that the interview had been excluded on these grounds and one expert had described it as 'flawless'. (See The Times, 23 November 1993, which had the headline, 'Acquittal puts police at war with lawyers'.) In this writer's view, there are bound to be wide differences in the perceptions of the various participants as to what is reasonable practice in this regard.

of this kind are not happening, and very few of the tapes are being played in court (Baldwin 1992b, pp. 20–3). This has meant that the courts are rarely in a position where they can pronounce on what is acceptable practice in the interview room and what is not.

The consequence is that interviewers and legal advisers operate in a sea of uncertainty. It is simply not possible for them to know for sure what conduct (short of physical violence or intimidation) the courts will be prepared to tolerate. Concepts such as 'coercion', 'impropriety', 'undue pressure' and 'oppression' are bandied about, but they have in practice no precise legal meaning. In the absence of firm rulings from the courts, such concepts inevitably remain largely in the eye of the beholder.

The Royal Commission on Criminal Justice could have provided a valuable service had it attempted to fill this void by promulgating a few guidelines of its own. In the writer's view, it was profoundly disappointing that the Commission did not attempt to advance a broad framework of guidelines or at least give some idea of what it considered to be fair and acceptable practice in this highly contentious area.[12] An independent and authoritative statement from the Commission on where it thought the balance between the parties should lie could have done much to resolve long-standing conflicts between police and lawyers whose exchanges would appear to have reached virtual stalemate. However, its report makes no real contribution to this discussion. Although the Commission acknowledged the lack of clarity in the present position, it was content (as has already been noted) for the professional bodies or the Home Office to sort things out themselves.

Legal advisers' role

Without some idea of the rules that should be applied, it is difficult to see how progress in improving interviewing standards can now be made. The factions are lined up and continue to adopt strong and contradictory positions on the key questions.[13] The history of relations between the police service and the Law Society is an unhappy one, and, in research that the author conducted for the Royal Commission into the role played by legal advisers in police stations (Baldwin 1992a, pp. 25–52), it was evident that many officers continue to

---

[12] See the response to this point from M. Zander (a member of the Royal Commission on Criminal Justice) (1993, p. 1339). The disagreement here relates to what can reasonably be expected of a Royal Commission. In the present writer's view, it was not a detailed code of practice that was expected of the Commission but a more general framework or at least some indication of what the rules of the game should be.

[13] Indeed, a prominent Law Society representative, Mr Anthony Edwards, has been reported as saying that the current attitude of the police is creating an atmosphere of 'trench warfare' with relations between police officers and solicitors deteriorating (*The Times*, 23 November 1993).

regard the presence of a legal representative as a threatening and hostile element in an interview. Despite the rethinking that PACE has produced, antagonism towards legal advisers remains strong throughout the police service. It is depressing to note how slowly these attitudes have changed over the years.

This is not to say that most legal advisers who present themselves at police stations are spoiling for a fight. Indeed, academic researchers who have observed legal advisers at interviews have not been greatly impressed by their performance.[14] In the writer's own research, advisers emerged as passive, if not silent, parties in most interviews in which they featured.[15] Two thirds of advisers said little, if anything, in interviews, and the videotapes of interviews that the author examined showed that most were note takers who sat quietly in a corner. Very few attempted to play what might be described as an interventionist role, no matter how an interview was conducted.

Worse, those advisers who intervened did so as often to facilitate the task of the police interviewers as to assist their clients. One minor, and unexpected, benefit of the video recordings is that they reveal which party is putting the questions. In some cases the lawyer's role is so conciliatory that it is not possible to tell from a tape recording whether a question has come from a police officer or from the lawyer. The videotapes also occasionally show conspiratorial glances being exchanged between police interviewers and legal advisers, and there was even one case in which the interviewer thanked the lawyer on tape for his assistance.

It might be argued that suspects in this situation would be better off with no legal adviser at all, because if a lawyer is present and makes no attempt to challenge the way an interview is being conducted, then the interviewers (and indeed the courts) might reasonably assume that no serious exception is being taken to it.[16] The difficulties posed by pusillanimous advisers are exacerbated by the fact that many firms of solicitors, faced with the relatively unattractive rates of remuneration from the legal aid fund for this work, have adopted the policy of sending articled clerks and other junior and unqualified staff to advise suspects in police stations (McConville and Hodgson 1993, ch. 2). It is obvious that such personnel are no match for an experienced police interrogator.

In his report to the Royal Commission, the present writer listed 15 cases (and could without difficulty have included more) where legal advisers sat in silence

---

[14] A good deal of research has been conducted on this question in the past 20 years, including two studies carried out under the auspices of the Royal Commission on Criminal Justice: see Baldwin 1992a and McConville and Hodgson 1993.

[15] Legal advisers were present at 182 of the 600 taped interviews (30.3%) that the writer examined.

[16] A dramatic illustration of the dangers to suspects in this situation was provided in the case of *R v Paris* (1993) 97 Cr App R 99.

throughout an interview when one would have expected some intervention from them (Baldwin 1992a, pp. 29–32). These examples included cases in which the interviewers blatantly assumed guilt from the very outset and failed to allow suspects a reasonable opportunity to put their side of the story; interviews in which technical legal points cropped up, and even ones in which serious arguments broke out between the officers and the suspect.

Although one should not assume that legal representatives ought to be intervening in interviews at every turn — and there are many circumstances in which they would be ill-advised to do so[17] — there was nonetheless no doubt in this writer's mind that much more could safely have been done by legal advisers to protect the interests of their clients and to check unfair police questioning. Their common posture is acquiescent and conciliatory, and it is evident in the new courses being introduced by the Law Society that a more strident approach is now being encouraged and fostered.

The difficulties that legal advisers face in adopting a more forceful role at interviews are, however, aggravated by the uncertainty that surrounds the rules to be followed. As with other features of the police interview, the role of legal advisers is not clearly defined. At present, it is police officers who have the upper hand at interviews, and this imbalance in the relative power of the parties is reinforced by Code of Practice C, para. 6.9, which states that a solicitor may even be required to leave the interview room 'if his conduct is such that the investigating officer is unable properly to put questions to the suspect'.[18] Note for guidance 6D further states that 'It is the duty of a solicitor to look after the interests of his client and to advise him without obstructing the interview'.

The Royal Commission rightly observed that the advice contained in this paragraph of the code of practice is unduly negative in tone, suggesting that a solicitor is 'an unwelcome obstruction to police inquiries and to be tolerated only as far as necessary' (1993, para. 54). However, perhaps an even greater difficulty, both for legal advisers and police interviewers, is that the code of practice represents such a jumble of inconsistencies that it makes the position of legal advisers uncertain, if not precarious, and the grounds for removing them from an interview room thoroughly ambiguous.

Police control of the interview

Such ambiguities have the effect of reinforcing police control of the interview. Legal advisers and their clients are bound to be at a disadvantage in a situation

---

[17]As is discussed below, there are strong incentives for suspects to cooperate at that stage, and rewards are offered to those who are compliant.
[18]This power to exclude troublesome lawyers from the interview room is one that is very rarely exercised.

in which it is police officers who decide when and where an interview takes place, how it is to be conducted and for how long. Interviews take place on police territory and on police terms.[19] Their power even to eject troublesome advisers from the interview room firmly underlines who is in charge.

The relatively weak position of legal advisers and the difficulties, uncertainties and doubts that surround their role are seen in sharp focus when they are deciding whether to advise suspects to remain silent at interview. While there is nothing improper about a lawyer advising silence at an interview (particularly if the details of the police evidence have not been disclosed at that stage, see McConville et al. 1991, ch. 3), it does not seem that such advice is given very frequently. The harsh reality is that in many cases a blanket refusal to answer police questions will simply not be in the suspect's own interests. The Law Society has itself stressed the 'substantial mitigating advantages generally of cooperation with the police',[20] and, since a considerable proportion of all criminal cases are dealt with by the police without referral to the Crown Prosecution Service, it is easy to see why. Competent legal advisers are aware of the benefits that can be derived from acting in an accommodating manner at that stage. About a third of all cases end as police cautions, for example, and, since this option is only available if suspects admit involvement in the offence in question, it acts in practice as a considerable disincentive to those suspects who might be inclined to stand upon their rights. It also operates in a similar way upon legal advisers who might encourage them to do so.[21]

These considerations place the legal adviser in a tricky situation, and it is by no means obvious that the most effective advisers are those who play the most confrontational (or adversarial) role. The government's moves in the Criminal Justice and Public Order Bill to restrict further the suspect's right to remain silent will, if implemented, exacerbate the lawyer's difficulties. Legal advisers daily face dilemmas as to what is the proper role to play at an interview, yet with so many of the fundamentals in doubt, there is no ready resolution to their difficulties. It is surely evident, however, that there is much more to it than mere training, which is what the Royal Commission saw as the main solution (1993, ch. 2). The critical questions remain unanswered. Are lawyers simply to act as referees to satisfy themselves that police questioning is fair to their clients? Or should they be solely concerned to push their clients' interests, if need be by advocating non-cooperation with police interviewers?

---

[19] Police officers can easily determine where suspects and their advisers sit in an interview room, and they may even deliberately prevent eye contact between legal advisers and their clients by physically bolting their seats to the floor.

[20] This emphasis was particularly strong in the 1988 version of the Law Society's handbook to solicitors.

[21] As several writers have noted, the law relating to the right of silence in this country is weak and equivocal; see, for example, Dixon 1991 and Easton 1991.

Before such issues can be confronted and these crucial questions answered with any degree of confidence, the many underlying dilemmas and uncertainties that surround police interviewing need first to be addressed. Despite a Royal Commission which regarded these issues as central, we are still a long way from answers.

References

Baldwin, J. (1992a), *The Conduct of Police Investigations* (Royal Commission on Criminal Justice Research Studies Nos. 2, 3 and 4) (London: HMSO).

Baldwin, J. (1992b), *Video Taping Police Interviews with Suspects: an Evaluation* (Police Research Series Paper 1) (London: Home Office Police Research Group).

Baldwin, J. (1993a), 'Police interviewing techniques: establishing truth or proof?', *British Journal of Criminology*, vol. 33, pp. 325–52.

Baldwin, J. (1993b), 'Power and police interviews', *New Law Journal*, vol. 143, pp. 1194–7.

Dixon, D. (1991), 'Politics, research and symbolism in criminal justice', *Anglo-American Law Review*, vol. 20, pp. 27–50.

Easton, S.M. (1991), *The Right to Silence* (Aldershot: Avebury).

Feldman, D. (1990), 'Regulating treatment of suspects in police stations: Judicial interpretation of detention provisions in the Police and Criminal Evidence Act 1984', *Criminal Law Review*, pp. 452–71.

Gudjonsson, G. (1992), *The Psychology of Interrogations, Confessions and Testimony* (Chichester: John Wiley).

McConville, M., and Baldwin J. (1982), 'The role of interrogation in crime discovery and conviction', *British Journal of Criminology*, vol. 22, pp. 165–75.

McConville, M., and Hodgson, J. (1993), *Custodial Legal Advice and the Right to Silence* ((Royal Commission on Criminal Justice Research Study No. 16) (London: HMSO).

McConville, M., Sanders, A., and Leng, R. (1991), *The Case for the Prosecution* (London: Routledge).

Moston, S., Stephenson, G.M., and Williamson, T.M. (1992), 'The effects of case characteristics on suspect behaviour during police questioning', *British Journal of Criminology*, vol. 32, pp. 23–40.

Royal Commission on Criminal Justice (1993), *Report* (Cm 2263) (London: HMSO).

Zander, M. (1993), 'Where the critics got it wrong', *New Law Journal*, vol. 143, pp. 1338–41.

5

Police Interviews with Juveniles

Roger Evans

Introduction

The Royal Commission on Criminal Justice was announced following the quashing by the Court of Appeal of the convictions for murder of the 'Birmingham Six'. The terms of reference of the Commission were wide-ranging, covering each stage in the criminal justice system from the investigation of an alleged offence through to appeals. Certain subjects fell outside these terms of reference including police powers of arrest and stop and search, sentencing policy and the legal definitions of criminal offences. The conduct of police interviews and the reliability of confession evidence were key concerns both in relation to the miscarriages of justice which led to the establishment of the Commission and for the Commission's research pro-gramme. Approximately a third of the research studies were concerned with the conduct of investigative interviews, the right to silence and confession evidence. A central issue is the degree to which the accused should be made a witting or unwitting instrument in his or her own conviction. Specifically the issue is 'to what extent the police may exploit the timidity, ignorance, lack of foresight and stupidity of the suspect in order to obtain a conviction' (Morris 1980).

The events that led to the establishment of the Commission concerned serious offences so naturally these were the main focus of the Commission's work. The majority of the Commission's recommendations are directed at the Crown Court rather than the magistrates' courts or youth courts. This chapter is concerned to summarise research on the conduct of police interviews with juveniles which was carried out for the Commission (Evans 1993a). The majority of juveniles are dealt with for minor offences by means of police cautioning or in the youth courts. In view of the Commission's focus on high-profile cases, involving serious offences, they needed to be convinced of the potential value of this research for furthering their understanding of how miscarriages of justice occur. The research is pertinent to the Commission's enquiry for two reasons.

First, juvenile suspects may be vulnerable in interviews because of their age. This is acknowledged by PACE Code of Practice C which requires that an appropriate adult should be present during the interview in order to protect the interests of the suspect and to facilitate communication (Code C, para 11.16). If the police use oppressive or persuasive interviewing techniques in order to obtain a confession from potentially vulnerable suspects, then this indicates that these techniques may be used as a matter of routine. They may not just be reserved for cases involving serious offences or hardened criminals with considerable experience of the criminal justice system.

Secondly, the majority of juveniles are now cautioned rather than taken to court. In 1992, for example, the average cautioning rate for England and Wales forces for 14–17-year-old males was 73% and for females 90%. Decisions about guilt and disposal, which were previously dealt with in open court, are now decided by the police, either acting alone or in consultation with other agencies. This represents a move from 'judicial' to 'administrative' justice (Pratt 1986). Power has been removed from the court to executive agencies. As a consequence decisions are taken in secret and opportunities for public control and scrutiny are reduced. Juvenile suspects are unlikely to be represented, either at the police station or at multi-agency panels or bureaux, and have no rights of appeal against a caution. As a consequence any miscarriages of justice which occur at the pre-court stage, as the result of police interviews, are unlikely to be disclosed or discovered. According to Home Office guidance, in force at the time of the research (Home Office Circular 14/1985), three conditions needed to be met before the police could caution a juvenile: the evidence must have been sufficient for there to have been a realistic chance of a conviction if the case had gone to court; suspects must have fully admitted their guilt; and parental consent to a caution must have been obtained. By focusing on spectacular miscarriages of justice the Commission were in danger of neglecting more routine practices which, given the widespread use of police cautioning, potentially affect a significant number of juveniles.

This chapter examines research into the conduct of police interviews with juveniles. It discusses the factors associated with admissions or denials, analyses the interview process and discusses the relationship between the content of interviews and police records of them. It considers the relationship between the research findings, the Commission's recommendations and subsequent changes in criminal justice policy. Whilst it does not directly address the issue of the right to silence, the evidence presented here suggests that a significant proportion of juvenile suspects would be well advised to take advantage of this right but that they are unlikely to be advised to do so by the parents, social workers or solicitor who attend their interviews.

Factors associated with admissions or denials

The Royal Commission on Criminal Justice research into the conduct of police interviews with juveniles was an extension of a study that followed a sample of 367 juveniles through the pre-court decision-making process in a single police force (Evans and Ferguson 1991). This research was based on one force in order to control for differences between forces in the prosecution process. The particular force was chosen because it included subdivisions served by the different types of inter-agency consultation systems typical of those found nationally; namely, a juvenile liaison panel and two bureaux. The sample consisted of all those juveniles arrested during the period the researchers were based in subdivisional police stations. Data were collected by interviewing arresting officers and custody sergeants, analysing crime files and observing inter-agency consultation discussions.

The Royal Commission on Criminal Justice research consisted of two parts. The first used the whole sample from the original research to conduct a statistical analysis of the factors associated with admissions or denials. The second part of the research was based on a sample of 164 tape-recorded interviews. These were selected because police records of the interview claimed that the suspects had confessed and the research aimed to examine the relationship between the conduct and content of interviews, the accuracy of police records and their relationship to disposals, particularly cautions.

The main conclusions from the statistical analysis include that suspects are more likely to confess when the evidence is strong and less likely when suspects have a criminal history or have committed a 'serious' offence. In one way this is hardly surprising as the consequences of a confession for the latter are likely to be more serious. Juvenile first offenders committing minor offences may expect to be cautioned, they may view this as a relatively light disposal, and may therefore readily confess. Admission rates remain high even when the evidence is weak, suggesting that juveniles may be more ready to confess than adults whatever the strength of the evidence. There is also some tentative evidence that confession rates vary with the police station where the interview took place. This may result from differences in interview techniques which are transmitted during the proces of socialisation into the culture of particular stations. Both this research, and that of Moston et al. (1992), provide important cumulative evidence that legal rather than non-legal variables are the main

79

determinants of the outcomes of interviews, the most statistically significant being the strength of evidence against the suspect.

These results have some theoretical significance for the thesis proposed in a recent and influential work by McConville et al. (1991). According to this account the outcomes of interviews are more likely to be the result of social processes than of any legal determinants such as the strength of evidence. It is argued that interviews are the main investigative strategy employed by the police, and in an adversarial justice system, a key site for the social construction of the case for the prosecution. The purpose of interviews is generally understood to be to elicit 'facts' from suspects but they also have to be understood in terms of the skill of the police in negotiating what the facts are. The concept of 'case construction' rests on the observation that the police select from the universe of facts available in ways which may be congruent with the law but may also be in pursuit of their own professional and occupational interests. McConville et al. (1991) claim the fact that the law is open textured and permissive explains the difference between the law in the books and the law in action. An arresting officer may form the opinion that a suspect is guilty early in the investigative process and may then use forms of questioning in interviews which enable the officer to claim that the suspect has confessed, or indeed which leads the suspect to confess, to an offence which he or she has not committed. The clear implication of this argument is that, whilst on occasions the police may act illegally, generally they do not need to do so in order to 'cook the books'. The open-textured nature of the law enables them to act in pursuit of their own interests in ways that are legal but not in the spirit of substantive law or the legal rhetoric of due process. Specifically in relation to interviews, the police rarely use simple information-seeking forms of questioning and tend to use persuasive interviewing techniques. These are inherently associated with unreliable confessions and social construction takes precedence over the influence of any relevant legal variables. Yet the main conclusion from the Evans (1993a) factor analysis is that legal variables, particularly the strength of evidence, are the main determinants of the outcomes of interviews.

Arrest, detention and their effect on vulnerability in interviews

Juvenile suspects, who may be vulnerable because of their age, may be rendered even more vulnerable by processes that occur prior to the interview. All the suspects in the sample were arrested indicating that this is a matter of routine. The police 'working rules' governing arrest relate to the general suspiciousness of suspects, the control of disorder, the influence of the status of victims on decisions to arrest and factors associated with the management of work-loads and time. The Royal Commission on Criminal Procedure (1981) acknowledged that arrest is a 'coercive power which may cause alarm and dismay'. Once arrested, juveniles are detained in police cells for up to four hours, although in some instances for considerably longer periods. This is usually while the police are waiting for appropriate adults, solicitors or social workers to arrive at the station. It is no surprise then that some suspects are in an anxious or suggestible state when they are interviewd. They may be keen to conclude the interview as soon as possible in order to obtain release. The Evans and Ferguson (1991) research noted that arresting officers reported that a significant proportion of juveniles were visibly afraid or distressed or cried at some point during arrest and detention. On the other hand, the more streetwise were described as totally lacking any respect for authority and showing no signs of concern, fear or remorse.

If a significant proportion of juveniles are 'alarmed and dismayed' by being arrested, and anxious to obtain release from the station, it might be expected that they would readily confess. The analysis of the sample of 164 taped interviews suggests that this is indeed the case as three quarters of the interviews are very brief with suspects confessing in the first sentence or two. A typical example is the case where, after the necessary preliminaries, the officer asked the suspect if he knew why he was being interviewed to which he replied: 'Because I done a burglary'. The majority (71.4%) of interviews took less than 15 minutes and the median length was around seven minutes. The fact that suspects readily confess is even more surprising in the light of the fact that in 38.5% of cases suspects were not told what they were accused of at any stage during the interview. Interviews might begin, 'Now we can get on with it. First of all you've been arrested, do you understand why? It's all about the school isn't it — this business with the school'. Suspects were left to give an account of what they thought they may have done in their own words. Even when suspects stated at the outset of the interview that they did not know why they were being questioned, interviewers typically responded with comments such as, 'Well you must have some idea'.

Questioning outside the formal interview

Immediate confessions, and the assumption that suspects knew what they were being accused of without being told, may also indicate that the formal interview had been rehearsed prior to their arrival at the station. There have been various estimates of the frequency of questioning outside the police station. Brown et al. (1993) suggest that this occurs in 10% of cases whilst Moston and Stephenson (1993) report that arresting officers say they have interviewed suspects before arrival at the station in 8% of cases. In contrast 31% of suspects reported that they had been questioned before their arrest. Questioning suspects at the scene of the crime, or whilst travelling to the station, provides opportunities for the police to offer inducements to confess. These may include the promise of early release, bail, threats to involve relatives or, particularly in the case of juveniles, other members of their peer group. The Commission's report (1993) noted the dangers of 'car-seat confessions' and the risk of invention by the police. Some officers were quite explicit about the desirability of rehearsal prior to formal interviews: 'I like to have a little chat to get things straight before I switch on the tape' (Evans and Ferguson 1991). There was also direct evidence from some interviews of prior discussion. For example, a suspect responded to questions about his movements within a building stating that: 'I didn't even go past the first office that you said the television was in' when up to this point in the interview there had been no mention of a television. In addition there are examples of parents, social workers and neighbours doing the police's job for them by questioning suspects and providing information, including information about alleged confessions. This may take place on the street or at the police station and may be fed into the formal interview.

The interview process

The interview is the principal investigative strategy used by the police (McConville et al. 1991) and the Commission's report notes with concern that interviews are often 'rambling, repetitious and insufficiently focused on the real issues'. A more serious criticism is that some interviewing officers too readily assume that the suspect is guilty and on occasions exert pressure that amounts to bullying or harassment in order to obtain a confession (Baldwin 1992). There is general agreement that obtaining a confession is one of the quickest routes to clearing up crime (Mawby 1979; Morris 1980; McConville and Baldwin 1981; McConville et al. 1991). Clear-up rates are an important measure of police efficiency. As many juvenile crimes are 'minor' (Parker et al. 1981; Evans and Ferguson 1991) clearing them up by obtaining confessions may be a relatively easy way of demonstrating efficiency.

Obtaining a confession also enables the police to avoid gathering other kinds of evidence, for example, witness statements or forensic evidence, and avoids unnecessary delays in disposing of juvenile cases so maximising any deterrent effect of the disposal. A confession recognises the rightness of the investigating officer's case, the soundness of his judgement and serves to reinforce perceptions of his skills and credibility amongst his colleagues (Laurie 1970). Whilst a confession is generally thought by police officers to be the sign of a 'good' interview, and by implication a 'good' interviewer (Moston et al. 1992), interviews may also serve other purposes. They may help to solve other crimes, recover stolen goods, and exonerate the innocent (Baldwin and McConville 1980).

Overtly oppressive tactics are not the only means of obtaining a confession when suspects do not readily admit to their guilt. Researchers have drawn attention to the more subtle persuasive interviewing techniques used by the police (Irving and McKenzie 1989; McConville and Hodgson 1993). Juvenile offenders frequently offend in groups which enables police interviewers to play suspects off against each other. For example, a common tactic is to imply that one of the other suspects has made a full confession so that it is only a matter of time before the truth comes out:

> We've spoken to Peter and we know that you're involved in it. We're not going to let it rest until we find out the truth so you might as well tell us now and get it off your chest. . . . Now I don't blame you for sticking out for what you have done because I would in the same circumstances, but we've got too much on you, mate, to let it stay as it is.

Other tactics include pointing out contradictions in the suspect's own account or between the suspect's account and that of witnesses, hinting that there is definite evidence to link the suspect to the offence, or telling suspects that owning up is a way of avoiding the police coming around to arrest and interview them again. One of the most notable features of police interviews with juveniles is that the police often do most of the talking with juveniles contributing the occasional 'Suppose so' or 'Dunno'.

McConville et al. (1991) suggest that the police 'rarely' rely on simple information-seeking forms of questioning and frequently rely on the use of persuasive tactics. Whilst they make a quantitative statement about the frequency of occurrence of events in interviews they largely rely on qualitative analysis, illustrating their arguments with selected case examples, without any discussion about the basis of their selection. Part of the purpose of the Evans (1993a) research was to see how frequently the police used particular types of tactics or forms of questioning. In 77% of the cases (N = 126) the police used simple information-seeking questions and suspects readily confessed, so casting doubt on the assertion that this 'rarely' occurs. (Moston et al. (1992) report a similar finding for their sample of interviews.) Persuasive tactics were used in the remaining 23% of cases and are more likely to be used when suspects do not readily confess (p = 0.001) or for more serious offences (p = 0.04).

Persuasive tactics are not necessarily successful in obtaining a confession. Examination of the outcomes of interviews suggests that persuasive tactics are just as likely to result in a denial or an admission that falls short of a full confession. According to the researcher's judgement of the outcome of the interview, rather than that recorded in the police summary, of the 38 cases where suspects did not immediately confess, 19 eventually confessed, 13 clearly denied the offence and in six cases there was no full confession or clear denial. In the 19 cases where suspects eventually confessed, the evidence against 12 was strong, four medium and three weak. This suggests that only a small number of suspects are persuaded to confess when the other evidence against them is weak.

The form of police questioning

Research is also concerned with forms of police questioning which are associated with unreliable confessions, particularly leading and legal closure questions (Gudjonsson and Clarke 1986; McConville et al. 1991; McConville and Hodgson 1993). Answers may be unwittingly influenced by messages contained in the questions. For example, leading questions suggest the answer in the wording: 'Was there a television in the room that you passed as you entered the building?'. Legal closure questions force information into a legally significant category in the hope that the suspect will adopt it. One example from the Evans and Ferguson (1991) research concerned a case where a boy briefly accepted a set of batteries handed to him in a shop by a friend. As soon as he realised that the friend might be intending to steal them, along with a video game, he handed them back and left the shop. In the interview he denied that he was present when any goods left the shop, any prior knowledge of the shoplifting or that he had any intention of becoming involved in it. When it was suggested to him that he had handled stolen goods he agreed that he must have and this was recorded as a 'full and frank' confession to shoplifting. As a legal concept, handling connotes knowledge that the goods were stolen. Thus, by exploiting the gulf between the legal meaning and the meaning which the boy attributed to handling, the interviewer obtained an apparent admission.

Leading questions were employed in 19.5% of the cases in the Evans (1993a) sample and legal closure questions in 12.2% of cases. Whilst these statistics might be indicative of attempts to exploit the suspects' interrogative suggestibility they cannot tell the whole story. This can be understood only in the context of the interview process as a whole. In some of the interviews there was clear evidence that, although suspects had initially denied being involved in any offence, they later accepted that they were by virtue of the persuasive logic of the interviewing officer.

The appropriate adult

Since juveniles are potentially vulnerable, PACE Code of Practice C requires that an appropriate adult should be present at the interview and provides guidance about his or her role:

Where the appropriate adult is present at an interview, he should be informed that he is not expected to act simply as an observer; and also that the purposes of his presence are, first, to advise the person being questioned and to observe whether or not the interview is being conducted properly and fairly, and, secondly, to facilitate communication with the person being interviewed. (PACE Code of Practice C, para. 11.16)

Researchers have noted that the role of the appropriate adult raises various difficulties and conflicts, for instance, advising suspects to exercise their right to silence may conflict with the requirement to facilitate communication (Thomas 1988; Dixon 1990). In 80% of cases in the sample of taped interviews, the appropriate adult was a non-professional, usually a parent although sometimes a relative or a friend. There was no evidence from the taped interview that they had been made aware of the PACE Code of Practice guidance and no way of knowing from the Evans and Ferguson (1991) research whether they had been advised of this prior to the interview. Brown et al. (1993) observed that it was extremely unusual for the custody officer to explain to the suspect what the role of the appropriate adult was. Three quarters of the appropriate adults made no contribution to the interview at all and those that spoke were as likely to be unsupportive as supportive of the children in their care. When parents colluded with the police in trying to obtain a confession they frequently used the type of abusive or oppressive tactics that are reminiscent of the worst police practices.

Although parents are generally passive observers of their children's interviews they contribute substantially more than professionals. Solicitors attended interviews in 11% of the cases and in half of these the police used persuasive tactics and obtained a confession. Brown et al. (1993) note that juveniles receive less information than adults about their rights and in their implementation. They are less likely to request legal advice than adults and there are very wide variations in the rate of requests between stations that cannot be explained in terms of the characteristics of the suspects.

Social workers, mainly residential or specialist juvenile justice workers, attended interviews in 18% of cases and in 62% of these the police used persuasive tactics and obtained a confession. There is only one example each of interviews in which either a social worker or a solicitor made any contribution whatsoever. They are either unaware of, ignore or are unable or unwilling to assert themselves in order to ensure that the police comply with PACE Code of Practice guidance on interviews with vulnerable suspects. In the case of social workers this is not surprising as they are very unlikely to have received any training on the law relating to appropriate adults or the skills required in this role as part of their basic professional qualification (Evans 1993b).

85

Records of interviews

The analysis of the taped interviews included an assessment of whether the suspect had clearly admitted, clearly denied or made an admission that fell short of a full confession to the offence that was the subject of the interview. A central concern here was to see whether there were cases where there was a clear denial, or at least no clear admission, that were nevertheless cautioned. There was no attempt to enter into complex legal judgements when making these assessments. In 13 of the sample of 164 cases the interview summary stated that the suspect had confessed when the suspect had clearly denied the offence, and in a further five cases the suspect had made an admission that fell short of a full confession. In 13 cases, the police record of the interview contained no clear statement about whether the juvenile had made a confession but an examination of the tapes revealed that he or she had clearly denied the offence.

The cases were tracked through the pre-court system until the point where a decision about disposal was taken. In 22% of those cases that were cautioned or informally warned, a closer examination of the interview suggests that, contrary to police records, suspects had either denied the offence or made an admission that falls short of a full confession. If this estimate was valid for all forces then in England and Wales in 1992, the latest year for which statistics are available, approximately 20,000 juveniles would have been cautioned for indictable offences despite the fact that they had not made a clear and reliable admission of the offence. This amounts to a considerable number of miscarriages of justice.

The Commission's response to the research

With respect to the question of interviewing outside the police station the Commission noted that the revised PACE Code of Practice (1991) attempts to distinguish between what constitutes an interview and other types of questioning. An interview is defined as questioning about suspect's involvement in an offence and should not occur outside a formal interview, whilst questioning to obtain information, an explanation of the facts, or in the ordinary course of an officer's duties is allowed. The Court of Appeal in *R* v *Cox* (1993) 96 Cr App R 464 has already said that this definition is contradictory and the Commission recommended that this confusion is clarified when Code C is next revised. It is difficult to see how questioning outside the formal interview situation can be avoided since the point at which an investigation turns into an accusation is not always clear. Juveniles, however, appear to be all too willing, no doubt encouraged by the informality of the situation, to volunteer damaging admissions, not necessarily in response to questioning, and without realising the implications. Second the Commission recommended that experiments with the use of tape recorders outside the station be continued. It is recognised that this would not be foolproof as a determined officer could put pressure on a suspect before the tape is turned on. Finally, the Commission recommended that suspects should be invited to comment on any alleged confession made outside the police station at the beginning of the tape-recorded formal interview.

The Commission noted that the Home Office has already taken steps to tackle the problems in investigative interviews by publishing new principles for their conduct and introducing a national training package (Home Office Circular 22/1992; Home Office Circular 7/1993). Prior to the publication of the Commission's report the Home Office had already made a plea for this issue to be left to themselves to resolve (Circular 22/1992); a plea which appears to have been accepted by the Commission. Despite the wealth of research evidence presented to it, the Commission simply commended the steps already taken by the Home Office and had nothing more to recommend concerning the conduct of police interviews.

With respect to appropriate adults, the Commission recommended that the Home Office should set up a comprehensive multidisciplinary review of their role, functions, qualifications, training and availability. The report suggests the possibility of establishing local panels of suitable people and questions why solicitors should not act as appropriate adults. It also raises the question of whether communications between appropriate adults and suspects should be privileged as communications with solicitors are.

In view of the evidence that the police frequently caution juveniles, even when the condition that they have made a full confession of guilt has not been met, the Commission displayed an uncritical enthusiasm for 'diversion'. The report commends the use of the caution as the principal means of achieving this, stating that moves towards a more liberal diversion policy would have the support of the police and the Crown Prosecution Service. It also recommends that cautioning should be placed on a statutory basis. It recommends that, if an offender is suffering from a 'mental disorder or social handicap', then it is desirable that a caution should be combined with a requirement to cooperate with social work agencies or the probation service or to agree to consult a doctor or attend a clinic. The probation service should take overall responsibility for this.

Events following the Commission's report

Since the Commission has reported criminal justice policy has undergone a series of dramatic reversals. Whereas the purpose of the Commission was to put in place mechanisms for preventing miscarriages of justice, the emphasis now is on increasing the efficiency of the criminal justice system. Some would argue that this shift from a 'civil libertarian' advocacy of 'suspects' rights' to 'a law and order' advocacy of 'crime control' is more apparent than real and in any case became the hidden agenda of the Royal Commission (Ericson 1993). Faced with a rising crime rate, and vociferous expressions of political and public concern, particularly from the right wing of the Conservative party, the Home Secretary has announced a 27-point package of law and order measures. This dismantles the carefully constructed reforms of the last decade which culminated in the Criminal Justice Act 1991. One of the main aims of this Act was to reserve custody for serious violent offenders but the Home Secretary has now announced that in his view, and in the absence of any evidence, prison works. As part of this package, and despite the recommendation of the Royal Commission, it is proposed to abolish the right to silence. Similarly new guidance has been issued to chief constables aimed at restricting the use of cautioning where the Commission recommended its extension (Home Office Circular 18/1994). Multiple cautions are discouraged on the grounds that they bring the disposal into disrepute. It has been calculated that this will increase the work-load of the already over-stretched youth court by some 40 per cent (Evans 1994). More pertinently, for the purposes of the argument here, if this Circular is fully implemented it is likely to reinforce more punitive attitudes towards cautioning amongst the police. This may in turn have the effect of making them more, rather than less, willing to assume guilt amongst juvenile suspects and in turn more casual about the determination of guilt during police interviews.

Conclusions

There are three main conclusions that can be drawn from this research and the Commission's response to it. First juvenile suspects rarely exercise their right to silence. Even when they are subject to the kind of oppressive or persuasive interview techniques that are associated with unreliable confessions they receive little help or guidance from appropriate adults, social workers or solicitors.

Secondly the Royal Commission's research studies contain a wealth of empirical, legal and theoretical material which suggests that there are fundamental problems with the conduct of police interviews. Yet there is little in the Royal Commission's report which addresses basic principles, attempts any theoretical understanding, or points to necessary legal reforms. The Commissioners chose instead to take a piecemeal and almost entirely pragmatic approach to the evidence presented to them. They have failed to make specific recommendations, preferring to leave it to the Home Office to introduce any reforms. This is the same Home Office that had responsiblity for policy on police interviews prior to the establishment of the Commission. It is hard to escape the conclusion that the Home Office officials who have been working with the Commission have successfully hijacked its agenda in this area.

Thirdly, there is evidence from this study that, contrary to Home Office guidance, a significant proportion of juveniles are cautioned even when they have either denied the offence or not clearly admitted their guilt. This represents a considerable number of miscarriages of justice and is an issue that has not been addressed either by the Commission or by subsequent events in criminal justice policy. The removal of the right to silence is further evidence of government's intention to shift attention away from concern with miscarriages of justice and towards achieving greater 'efficiency' in terms of convictions. There is plenty of evidence from this research that vulnerable juvenile suspects are not adequately protected during the course of police interviews.

References

Baldwin, J. (1992) *Video Taping Police Interviews with Suspects: An Evaluation* (Police Research Series Paper No. 1) (London: Home Office, Police Research Group).

Brown, D., Ellis, T., and Larcombe, K. (1993), *Changing the Code: Police Detention under the Revised PACE Codes of Practice* (Home Office Research Study 129) (London: HMSO).

Dixon, D. (1990), 'Juvenile suspects and the Police and Criminal Evidence Act', in Freeston, D. (ed.), *Children and the Law* (Hull University Press).

Ericson, R. (1993), 'The Royal Commission on Criminal Justice system surveillance'. Paper presented to the Criminal Justice in Crisis conference, University of Warwick, September, 1993.

Evans, R. (1993a), *The Conduct of Police Interviews with Juveniles* (Royal Commission on Criminal Justice Research Study No. 8) (London: HMSO).

Evans, R. (1993b), 'The social work role in police interviews', *Community Care* (25 November).

Evans, R. (1994), 'Cautioning: counting the cost of retrenchment' to be published in *Criminal Law Review*.

Evans, R., and Ferguson, T. (1991), *Comparing Different Juvenile Cautioning Systems in One Police Force Area*. Report to the Home Office Research and Planning Unit.

Gudjonsson, G., and Clark, N. (1986), 'Suggestibility in police interrogation: a social psychological model', *Social Behaviour*, vol. 1, p. 83.

Irving, B., and McKenzie, I. (1989), *Police Interrogation: the effects of the Police and Criminal Evidence Act 1984* (London: Police Foundation).

Laurie, P. (1970), *Scotland Yard* (London: Bodley Head).

Mawby, R. (1979), *Policing the City* (Farnborough: Saxon House).

McConville, M., and Baldwin, J. (1981), *Courts, Prosecution and Conviction* (Oxford: Clarendon Press).

McConville, M., and Hodgson, J. (1993), *Custodial Legal Advice and the Right to Silence* (Royal Commission on Criminal Justice Research Study No. 16) (London: HMSO).

McConville, M., Sanders, A., and Leng, R. (1991), *The Case for the Prosecution: Police Suspects and the Construction of Criminality* (London: Routledge).

Morris, P. (1980), *Police Interrogation: Review of Literature* (Royal Commission on Criminal Procedure Research Study No. 3) (London: HMSO).

Moston, M., and Stephenson, G.M. (1993), *The Questioning and Interviewing of Suspects outside the Police Station* (Royal Commission on Criminal Justice Research Study No. 22) (London: HMSO).

Moston S., Stephenson, G.M., and Williamson, T. (1992), 'The effects of case characteristics on suspect behaviour during police questioning', *British Journal of Criminology*, vol. 32, pp. 23–40.

Parker, H., Casburn, M., and Turnbull, D. (1981), *Receiving Juvenile Justice* (Oxford: Blackwell).

Pratt, J. (1986), 'Diversion from the juvenile court', *British Journal of Criminology*, vol. 26, pp. 212–33.

Royal Commission on Criminal Justice (1993), *Report* (Cm 2263) (London: HMSO).

Royal Commission on Criminal Procedure (1981), *Report* (Cmnd 8092) (London: HMSO).

Thomas, T. (1988), 'The Police and Criminal Evidence Act 1984: the social work role', *Howard Journal of Criminal Justice*, vol. 27, p. 256.

6

Psychological Vulnerability: Suspects at Risk

Gisli H. Gudjonsson

Current legal provisions in England

The law regarding confession evidence in England is currently governed by the Police and Criminal Evidence Act 1984 (PACE) which came into force in January 1986.

Under PACE, s. 66, five codes of practice, referred to as Codes A, B, C, D and E have been issued. These act as guidance to the police about procedure and the treatment of suspects. The codes have legislative power insofar as breach of them may result in evidence, including confession evidence, being ruled inadmissible. The most innovative aspects of these codes, as far as confession evidence is concerned, relate to the introduction of tape recording of interviews and the use of 'appropriate adults' during interviews in order to strengthen the reliability and fairness of confession evidence.

Although PACE has not been revised since its implementation in 1986, the Home Office has published a revised version of the codes of practice which came into force on 1 April 1991. Procedural changes have been made in the codes which affect police officers at all levels (Metropolitan Police 1991). Code C, Code of Practice for the Detention, Treatment and Questioning of Persons by Police Officers, is the most relevant to the protection of suspects whilst being detained at police stations.

The legal issues concerning the admissibility of confession evidence are principally determined by ss. 76 and 78 of PACE, but s. 82(3) is also sometimes used when the other two sections have failed (Birch 1989). According to Richardson (1993), PACE replaced the common law on improperly obtained confessions (s. 76) and evidence (s. 78), whilst retaining the power given to the courts in common law to exclude any evidence at their discretion.

Sections 76 and 78 are the legal tests most commonly applied to cases in practice (Gudjonsson 1992a, 1992b). There is a fundamental difference between these two sections which relates to discretionary powers: s. 76 involves 'proof of facts', whereas s. 78 involves 'the exercise of judgement by the court' (Birch 1989, p. 96). Another difference is the emphasis in s. 76 on police behaviour and the reluctance of judges to include under this provision unreliability due solely to internal factors (e.g., drug withdrawal, disturbed mental state). There is generally the need to establish some kind of impropriety to operate s. 76, although this is not invariably the case (Gudjonsson 1994).

Inherent psychological factors, such as a suspect's disturbed mental state or learning disabilities, are principally relevant to inadmissibility under s. 78, where it may be considered unfair to the defence, in view of the circumstances of the case, to allow the evidence to go before the jury.

Section 77(1) of PACE deals with confessions obtained from persons who suffer from mental handicap (now commonly referred to as 'learning disabilities'). In cases of learning disabilities, the court must warn the jury that there is special need for caution before convicting the accused solely on the basis of his or her confession. No similar provision is offered in PACE for persons who suffer from other types of mental disorder, such as mental illness. There is, however, a general protection for persons suffering from 'mental disorder', which is described in detail in Code of Practice C. The definition used for 'mental disorder' is the same as in the Mental Health Act 1983, and means 'mental illness, arrested or incomplete development of mind, psychopathic disorder and any other disorder or disability of mind' (Code C, note for guidance 1G).

Code C provides protection concerning the interviewing of 'special groups', such as foreigners who have problems with the English language, juveniles, those who are hard of hearing, and persons who are mentally disordered. Where there is a language problem, an interpreter must be called to assist. The relevant legal provision for other 'special groups' includes: 'A juvenile or a person who is mentally disordered or mentally handicapped, whether suspected or not, must not be interviewed or asked to provide or sign a written statement in the absence of the appropriate adult' (Code C, para. 11.14).

An 'appropriate adult' is a responsible adult called in by the police in order to offer special assistance to the detainee. The appropriate adult can be a relative of the detainee or a professional person such as a social worker or a psychologist. The detainee's solicitor cannot act as an appropriate adult (Code C, note for guidance 1F). Gudjonsson (1993) has raised concerns about using relatives as appropriate adults, because their objectivity may be overriden by emotions and sometimes they suffer from problems (e.g., learning disabilities) which are not immediately obvious to the police.

The role of the appropriate adult is: 'to advise the person being questioned and to observe whether or not the interview is being conducted properly and fairly, and, secondly, to facilitate communication with the person being interviewed' (Code C, para. 11.16). This means that the role of the appropriate adult is an active one (i.e., he or she is not acting simply as an observer).

Persons with mental disorder are considered 'vulnerable' or 'at risk', because:

> ... they may, without knowing or wishing to do so, be particularly prone in certain circumstances to provide information which is unreliable, misleading or self-incriminating. Special care should therefore always be exercised in questioning such a person, and the appropriate adult should be involved, if there is any doubt about a person's age, mental state or capacity. Because of the risk of unreliable evidence it is also important to obtain corroboration of any facts admitted whenever possible. (Code C, note for guidance 11B.)

According to Gudjonsson (1993), there are two major problems with PACE and the codes of practice in connection with the generic term 'mental disorder'. First, no operational definition is given of what precisely constitutes mental disorder. This poses problems for police officers, who are expected to be able to identify persons suffering from a condition which is not properly defined or described in their codes of practice. Secondly, the codes of practice do not indicate how certain characteristics, such as mental illness or mental handicap, place suspects 'at risk'. The assumption seems to be that mental disorder places these persons at risk in the sense that they may unintentionally provide the police with unreliable accounts of events, including a false confession, because they may not fully comprehend the importance of the questions put to them or the implications of their answers, or that they are unduly influenced by immediate gains and police pressure.

The police are responsible for identifying persons who are at risk and have to find a suitable person to act in the capacity of an appropriate adult. Typically, in the case of juveniles, the police will ask a relative to act as an appropriate adult, whereas with adult interviewees they commonly obtain a social worker.

Psychological vulnerabilities

There are two main issues typically addressed by psychologists and psychiatrists which are relevant to the admissibility and reliability of self-incriminating admissions. These are:

(a)   Was the defendant, due to psychological vulnerability, entitled to the presence of an appropriate adult during the police interview?

(b)   Are there any psychiatric or psychological grounds on which to challenge the admissibility and reliability of the confession?

In this context, psychological vulnerability can be construed to mean psychological characteristics or mental states which:

(a)   impair suspects' ability to understand their legal rights,

(b)   render suspects prone, in certain circumstances, to provide information which is unreliable or misleading.

Assessments of vulnerability are best viewed as falling into three distinct groups. The first group can be labelled 'mental disorder', the second, 'abnormal mental state', and the third, 'personality characteristics'. Let us look at each of these in turn.

Mental disorder

'Mental disorder' implies that the person suffers from diagnosable mental problems, such as *mental illness* (e.g., schizophrenia, depressive illness), *learning disability*, or *personality disorder*. Personality disorder became important legally in England in connection with disputed confessions in the case of Judith Ward, who was wrongfully convicted of terrorist crimes in 1974 and had her conviction overturned by the Court of Appeal in 1992 (*R* v *Ward* [1993] 1 WLR 619; Mills 1992a; 1992b).

Abnormal mental state

People can suffer from an abnormal mental state whilst in police custody without having had a history of mental disorder. For example, in our recent study for the Royal Commission on Criminal Justice, which will be discussed in detail below, we found that about 20% of the suspects were reporting an abnormally high level of anxiety, yet only about 7% were suffering from mental illness, such as schizophrenia or depressive illness.

In addition to high generalised anxiety, and sometimes independent of it, suspects may suffer from specific phobic anxiety, such as claustrophobia (e.g., exaggerated fear of being locked up in a confined space like a police cell) or panic attacks. In our Royal Commission study, extreme fear of being locked up in a police cell was very rare (we found only one case out of 171) although many detainees complained that they were distressed about being locked up at the police station.

Some suspects who are interviewed by the police are in a state of bereavement, because of loss of a loved one. This may, on occasions, render them vulnerable to giving misleading self-incriminating statements because of feelings of guilt and distress that typically accompany the condition.

Suspects who are high on drugs, or are withdrawing from drugs, are increasingly being arrested and interviewed by the police. Some drug addicts may be vulnerable to giving erroneous accounts of events when asked leading questions and placed under interrogative pressure.

Finally, some medical conditions (e.g., cardiovascular problems, diabetes, epilepsy) may result in a disturbed or abnormal mental state whilst the person is at the police station.

Personality characteristics

A number of personality characteristics may be important when evaluating the reliability of self-incriminating admissions. The three most extensively researched variables are suggestibility, compliance and acquiescence (Gudjonsson 1992a). More recently the present author has been researching into the importance of 'confabulation' (Clare and Gudjonsson 1993).

'Suggestibility' refers to the tendency of people to give in to leading questions and interrogative pressure. It can be measured by the use of a behavioural test, like the Gudjonsson Suggestibility Scales (Gudjonsson 1984; 1987), where people are systematically misled in an experimental way and their responses are carefully monitored and compared with those of relative normative groups for comparison purposes. If the scores obtained are statistically infrequent, that is, they occur in fewer than 5% of the general population then the person can be described as being abnormally suggestible on the test (Gudjonsson 1992a).

The concept of 'compliance' overlaps, to a certain extent, with suggestibility, but it is more associated with eagerness to please and the tendency to avoid conflict and confrontation. Compliance is more difficult to measure by behavioural observation than suggestibility and is typically measured by a self-report questionnaire. This makes it a measure that is easier to fake than measures of suggestibility.

'Acquiescence' refers to the tendency of people, when in doubt, to answer questions in the affirmative irrespective of content. The main reason for this tendency is that they answer questions in the affirmative without properly listening to them or fully understanding them. Acquiesence is more closely correlated with low intelligence than either suggestibility or compliance (Gudjonsson 1992a).

'Confabulation' refers to people filling in gaps in their memory with imagined material (Gudjonsson 1992a). Confabulation appears to be particularly strong in some cases of personality disorder, as it was in the cases of Joe Giarratano (Gudjonsson 1992a) and Judith Ward (Mills 1992a; 1992b).

Personality characteristics, such as suggestibility, compliance and acquiescence, are not relevant to the assessment of all cases of alleged false confessions. Suggestibility and compliance are only relevant if the police asked leading questions or placed the person under pressure in some way. Acquiescence is most relevant when a person seems to have given affirmative answers to questions that he or she may not have fully understood.

Juveniles have been shown to be particularly susceptible to interrogative pressure during interviewing (e.g., to negative feedback and repeated questioning), even though they do not yield any more readily to leading questions than adults (Gudjonsson and Singh 1984; Singh and Gudjonsson 1992). This important vulnerability of juvenile witnesses to interrogative pressure is typically overlooked by leading experts on child witnesses (e.g., see Dent and Flin 1992).

In order to understand what psychological vulnerabilities are pertinent to a given case it is important to conduct a comprehensive assessment. However, the expert has to have some idea of what are the most relevant factors to assess. The assessment has to be focused on the relevant issues and suspected vulnerabilities. In many cases no relevant vulnerabilities are found. The fact that a vulnerability is found does not mean that the defendant may have made a false confession. When vulnerabilities are found they will need to be interpreted and placed within the context of the case and other relevant evidence. This is often the most difficult task and requires considerable experience and detailed knowledge about the case.

Vulnerabilities mean that under certain circumstances, suspects may give a confession which cannot be relied upon and special caution is therefore required when eliciting information from them. Even when vulnerabilities are severe, they do not invariably or necessarily result in an unreliable statement. Gudjonsson (1992c) discusses how different types of vulnerability may make people vulnerable to psychologically distinct types of false confession, such as 'coerced-internalised', 'coerced-compliant' and 'voluntary'.

Some suspects may have limited understanding of their legal rights whilst in police custody, which can potentially undermine their ability to make informed decisions and to give a reliable statement to the police.

Understanding the 'Notice to Detained Persons'

Background to the Royal Commission study

PACE Code C stipulates that a person who is under arrest and brought to a police station must be informed of his or her legal rights. These are the right to have somebody informed of his or her arrest, the right to consult with a solicitor, the right to consult the codes of practice, and the right to have a copy of the custody record. These rights do not have to be exercised immediately after the detainee is told of them (i.e., they can be exercised at any time whilst the person is detained at the police station).

After explaining these rights to the detainee, the custody officer must give the arrested person a written leaflet which explains in detail their rights. This is known as the 'Notice to Detained Persons'. At the top of the leaflet is a police caution which states: 'If you are asked questions about a suspected offence you do not have to say anything unless you wish to do so, but what you say may be given in evidence'.

Gudjonsson (1990a; 1991) was concerned about the apparent reading complexity of the original notice and set out to analyse its complexity by two different methods. First, the paragraphs in the notice were analysed for reading complexity by using the Flesch Formula for Reading Ease (Flesch 1948). Secondly, there was also an exploratory study of 15 convicted offenders with IQs below 100, who were specially tested with regard to their understanding of the notice.

The results from Flesch Formula analyses indicated that fewer than one in four people in the general population would fully understand the notice. The exploratory study indicated that the great majority of people with IQs below 100 would be unable to understand all the sentences in the notice, even when instructed to study each question carefully in a relaxed setting. Gudjonsson concluded that the Notice to Detained Persons was far too complicated for most offenders to understand and it needed to be rewritten in much simpler language. Clare and Gudjonsson (1992b) came to a similar conclusion in a study exploring the recall and understanding of the caution and rights in police detention by persons of average intellectual ability and persons with a mild mental handicap.

The findings from the Gudjonsson study were originally published in the *Law Society's Gazette* (Gudjonsson 1990a), which resulted in the Home Office promising publicly to simplify the Notice to Detained Persons (Dyer 1990). This was done with the introduction of the revised codes of practice, which came into effect on 1 April 1991.

Gudjonsson et al. (1992) set out to analyse the revised notice using a similar methodology to that of Gudjonsson 1991. In the new notice the number of sentences used had been increased from 10 to 24 (with the police caution and information provided before the four main headings there are 29 sentences in total in the new notice). In particular, the section of the notice concerned with the right to legal advice had been altered from two sentences to 14 sentences.

The Flesch analyses carried out on the new Notice to Detained Persons showed certain improvements on the original notice, particularly in relation to

97

free legal advice, but the document as a whole was still considered far too difficult to read and understand for people of below-average intelligence. This is confirmed by the exploratory study of 31 subjects with IQs between 60 and 128, who had been asked to explain the meaning of each sentence in the notice. The results indicate that the great majority of persons of average intelligence or below are likely to find many of the sentences in the new notice too difficult to comprehend.

Therefore, the Home Office had been partly successful in simplifying the Notice to Detained Persons, but overall the document remained far too complicated for the majority of persons to understand fully.

The Royal Commission study (Clare and Gudjonsson 1992)

Clare and Gudjonsson (1992a) developed an 'experimental' notice to detained persons, the direction of which was guided by the previous studies into the two official notices. The objective was to develop a notice which was much simpler than the current notice. In addition, the research aimed to overcome the apparent reluctance of some groups of vulnerable persons (e.g., those with a mental handicap) to spontaneously identify themselves as requiring special assistance from an appropriate adult.

In the experimental notice the police caution and the four other main rights were translated into simple everyday language. The notice was presented in a three-section format, which contained:

(a)   a section for custody officers to read out, which gave information on the caution and other rights (referred to as 'verbal information section') and also contained questions to encourage detainees to identify themselves as needing special help because of reading problems, learning disabilities, attendance at a special school or mental illness;

(b)   a leaflet with further information about the detainees' rights (referred to as a 'further information leaflet'); and

(c)   a 'laminated card', outlining the main points of the information.

The three sections were analysed in the same way as the original and current notices had been. The Flesch Formula showed a marked improvement, with the further information leaflet having a score of 77 in contrast to 50 in the original notice and 56 in the current notice. The section on the laminated card had a Flesch score of 84 and the verbal information section for the custody officers had a score of 84. Combining all three sections gave a Flesch score of 80. This compared very favourably with the reading ease of the best-selling English daily tabloid newspaper, the *Sun*, which has a Flesch score of about 70.

Therefore, Clare and Gudjonsson were able to produce a notice which was written even more simply than articles in the *Sun*.

One hundred adults took part in the piloting of the experimental notice. The mean IQ score of the 100 subjects was 79.5 (standard deviation 16, range 60–128). All subjects were asked to explain the meaning of each sentence in the three-section format. This was identical to the analyses conducted on the original (Gudjonsson 1990a; 1991) and current (Gudjonsson et al. 1992) notices.

Overall, 72% of the experimental notice was understood by all subjects, compared with only 59 and 41% of the original and current notices, respectively.

The self-reporting of needing special help was endorsed by 54 (54%) of the subjects; 15 subjects did so exclusively on the grounds that they had mental illness problems or had attended a special school. The remaining 39 subjects identified themselves as having reading problems and/or learning difficulties, which were corroborated on psychological testing in all but two of the cases. This indicates a very low false positive error rate. Out of all subjects with IQ scores of 75 or below or a reading age of less than nine years, 80% had identified themselves as needing special help.

Psychological vulnerability study

Background to the Royal Commission study

There have been very few attempts made to study the psychological vulnerabilities of suspects detained at police stations. The impetus for the Royal Commission study had come from the important observation work conducted at Brighton Police Station by Irving (1980) and Irving and McKenzie (1989). There were three separate studies, conducted in 1979, 1987 and 1988. In the first study (Irving 1980), Irving observed 60 suspects immediately prior to and during their being interviewed by the police. Sixteen (26%) were judged to be either intoxicated (18%) or mentally ill (8%). Many others were considered to be in an abnormal mental state due to distress concerning their custody and interrogation. In total, 25 (42%) of the suspects were viewed by Irving to be in some way mentally disturbed during the police interview.

Irving and McKenzie (1989), in two replication studies, observed 136 suspects, 68 in each of the years 1986 and 1987. The number of suspects who were judged as being in an 'abnormal' mental state dropped to 21 (31%) and 9 (13%) for the years 1986 and 1987, respectively. The main explanation for the improvement in mental state during interviewing appears to relate to fewer suspects being interviewed when they were visibly under the influence of alcohol as a result of the implementation of the Police and Criminal Evidence Act.

The main difference between the original and replication studies is that in the former Irving was the only observer whereas in the replications McKenzie was the principal observer. Irving and McKenzie appear to have taken great care to ensure consistency in their observations and recordings. Therefore, the change of the observer may have had little or no effect on the results, although this possibility cannot be ruled out.

In the three studies, which comprise a total of 196 subjects, only one suspect (0.5%) was judged to be mentally handicapped. This appears to be an artificially deflated figure and indicates that there may be serious difficulties involved in identifying, by behavioural observation alone, persons with a mental handicap prior to their being interviewed by the police.

Gudjonsson (1990a) compared the IQ scores of 98 alleged false confessors and 74 other forensic referrals. The two groups were found to have Full Scale IQs of 80 and 91, respectively. These results indicate that a significant proportion of suspects interviewed at police stations would be likely to be suffering from a significant intellectual impairment. The implication is that the studies of Irving and McKenzie, which estimated the extent of mental abnormality through observation rather than psychometric testing, have underestimated the incidence of significant intellectual impairment among suspects interviewed at police stations.

The Royal Commission study (Gudjonsson et al. 1993)

The purpose of the Royal Commission study was to extend the observational studies of Irving and McKenzie by formally assessing suspects detained at police stations for questioning. Three clinical psychologists (Clare, Gudjonsson and Rutter), attended two police stations in the South East of England (Peckham in South London and Orpington in Kent), over a period of four months, and assessed 173 suspects. A further 24 detainees refused to participate in the study. Of the 173 assessments commenced, 144 (83%) were males and 124 (73%) were Caucasian. Each assessment typically lasted between 45 minutes and one hour. Nine of the assessments could not be completed for various reasons, but mainly because the police interrupted the session and wanted to interview the detainee.

The assessment consisted of an initial interview, where the detainees' mental state, background, and understanding of their legal rights, were assessed, which was followed by psychological testing of intellectual and reading ability, anxiety proneness, and interrogative suggestibility.

The main findings can be classified under two headings: (a) results from interview and observation; and (b) results from psychological testing.

Results from interview and observation

Seventy per cent of the detainees reported being unemployed. A similar number (71%) claimed to have previous convictions, with about a third (36%) having served a prison sentence.

~~One third (33%) reported having consumed alcohol within 24 hours of arrest,~~ with the corresponding figure for illicit drug taking being 22%.

The mental state of the detainees during the seven days preceding their arrest varied considerably. Only two reported having heard voices, whereas sleep disturbance (38%), loss of appetite (21%), and feeling low in mood (43%) were common. A small minority (9%) reported having had suicidal thoughts and feelings.

The assessment of the detainees' mental state at the police station indicated that 7% were mentally ill, the primary diagnoses being schizophrenia and depressive illness. Twenty-one detainees (12%) appeared to be in a highly agitated state, two appeared intoxicated, and 12 (7%) looked drugged.

The researchers identified only four detainees (3%) as being obviously mentally handicapped.

On the basis of the mental-state assessment, the researchers considered that there were good clinical reasons for the presence of an appropriate adult in 25 (15%) of the cases where detainees were subsequently interviewed by the police. The police called in an appropriate adult in only seven (4%) of the cases. All were from the group of 25 detainees considered by the researchers in need of an appropriate adult. A forensic medical examiner (previously known as 'police surgeon') was called in by the police to see 26 (16%) detainees, which was primarily for a medical rather than a psychiatric reason.

Results from psychological testing

The intellectual functioning of the detainees was assessed by their scores on three subtests of the WAIS-R (Wechsler 1981), which were vocabulary, comprehension and picture completion. These subtests were chosen because they gave the best general indication of the detainees' intellectual abilities and were least likely to be affected by stress of the arrest and confinement.

The mean IQ for the suspects was only 82, with the range 61–131. Almost 9% of the sample had a prorated IQ score below 70, compared with about 2% of the general population, one third (34%) had a prorated IQ score of 75 or below (i.e., bottom 5% of the general population).

It is likely that, to a certain extent, the IQ scores obtained represent an underestimate of the detainees' intellectual abilities due to the circumstances and context of testing, but the findings nevertheless highlight the fact that the police are commonly interviewing persons of low intellectual abilities.

101

The detainees' reading ability was measured by the Schonell Graded Word Reading Test (Schonell and Goodacre 1974). The sample obtained a mean score of 74, which gives an average reading age of 11 years and 8 months. Only 6.5% of the sample obtained a score of below 43, which represents a reading age of 9 years and can be described as functional illiteracy.

Anxiety was tested by the use of the State-Trait Anxiety Inventory (STAI) (Spielberger 1983). Trait anxiety, refers to relatively stable individual differences in anxiety proneness whereas state anxiety is the intensity of feelings of anxiety at a particular point in time (e.g., whilst at the police station).

The mean trait anxiety score (44.6) obtained for the sample as a whole was similar to that typically found among prison inmates, whereas the mean state anxiety score (53.6) was highly elevated. About 20% of the detainees had a state anxiety score above 65, which falls in the 95th percentile rank for prison inmates (Spielberger et al. 1970).

Interrogative suggestibility was measured by the Gudjonsson Suggestibility Scale (GSS 2) (Gudjonsson 1987). The detainees' immediate (11.3) and delayed (10.2) recall and their total suggestibility (11.6), were similar to forensic populations of comparable intellectual capacity (Gudjonsson 1990b). Therefore, the fact that they were assessed at the police station, under stressful conditions, may not have adversely influenced their ability to resist suggestions and cope with interrogative pressure.

With regard to suggestibility, it is noteworthy that the Caucasian detainees were significantly less suggestible than the Afro-Caribbean detainees, even after differences in memory scores had been controlled for (Gudjonsson et al. 1994).

Conclusions and implications

It is evident that the current Notice to Detained Persons is still far too complicated and needs to be revised and simplified, along the lines recommended by Clare and Gudjonsson. Indeed, the Royal Commission (see Royal Commission on Criminal Justice 1993, p. 34) recommended that the notice developed and piloted by Clare and Gudjonsson be tested in real-life conditions at police stations.

The research by Clare and Gudjonsson shows that the Notice to Detained Persons can be written in much simpler language than the current version without losing its legal requirements. Indeed, the experimental version proved easier to read than the *Sun* newspaper. It is unlikely that the notice could be simplified any more without losing its legal acceptability and basic terminology. Nevertheless, there were still subjects who had problems understanding some of the sentences and these people were almost invariably intellectually disadvantaged. The experimental notice appears to maximise the number of people who understand the majority of sentences in the notice. It is unlikely that a notice could ever be constructed that would be fully understood by all suspects detained at police stations.

The results show that asking subjects to state if they need special help was effective in identifying 80% of those who proved to be vulnerable on psychological testing, whilst having a very low false positive error rate. The implication is that more vulnerable detainees could be identified at police stations if the police were to adopt the method developed by Clare and Gudjonsson of asking detainees if they fulfilled the requirements for special help. This could form a part of the booking-in procedure where custody officers encourage detainees to declare their vulnerabilities.

The identification of psychological problems by the police prior to interviewing is desirable, because it helps them ensure that suspects who are at risk are provided with the necessary legal protection in accordance with the PACE codes of practice. It is evident from the study that the police called in an appropriate adult only in exceptional circumstances, but interestingly they were able to detect all the most disabled and vulnerable detainees and provided them with the presence of an appropriate adult.

The results of the study demonstrate that the low IQ of many of the detainees was not immediately apparent to the police or the clinicians on brief acquaintance. This concurs with the experience of Gudjonsson (1992a) that in forensic practice it is typically difficult to identify intellectually disadvantaged individuals without formal psychological testing.

A similar problem arose with regard to the diagnosis of depression. There were a few severely depressed detainees, whose condition was not apparent without a clinical interview.

Police officers and forensic medical examiners should be provided with basic training in how to identify vulnerable interviewees. In addition, police officers should be provided with training in how to interview people to maximise the relevance, completeness and reliability of the information obtained. Special training is required for interviewing those who are at risk; once identified as being at risk the police should exercise special caution when interviewing them (e.g., phrasing questions simply, avoiding leading questions, and ensuring that they are not placing them under undue pressure), because it increases the likelihood that information obtained during interviewing is reliable and will not be ruled inadmissible when the case goes to trial. This serves the purpose of reducing the likelihood that a miscarriage of justice will occur (either a wrongful conviction or the freeing of a guilty defendant because of legal technicality).

There is an urgent need for a comprehensive review of the role, function, qualification, training, effectiveness and availability of persons acting as an appropriate adult. It is arguable that only qualified persons should act as an appropriate adult. There are various reasons why relatives may be unsuited to this role (Gudjonsson 1993). Eventually, special guidelines should be produced for persons acting in the capacity of an appropriate adult which clearly outline their duties and responsibilities.

What implications do the findings have for the right to silence? The right to silence means that a suspect's decision to refuse to answer questions cannot be used subsequently against him or her by the jury. Conversely, abolishing the right to silence means that the prosecutor and the judge can invite the jury to draw adverse inferences from the suspect's silence when interviewed by the police or at trial. Various arguments have been put forward for and against the right to silence and these were recently comprehensively reviewed by the Royal Commission on Criminal Justice (1993). The findings from our two Royal Commission studies highlight the various psychological vulnerabilities of suspects detained at police stations. For example, the low level of intelligence among many suspects, in addition to various other psychological vulnerabilities, suggests that, were the right of silence to be abolished, some suspects: (a) may feel under undue pressure to make self-incriminating admissions which they do not wish to make; (b) may not fully understand the likely legal implications if they remain silent at the police station. Abolishing the right to silence increases the complexity of decision making required of detainees. Considering that many detainees are of low intelligence this may place some at increased disadvantage in not being able to make informed decisions. What is needed is proper research into the effects of abolishing the right of silence.

References

Birch, D. (1989), 'The PACE hots up: confessions and confusions under the 1984 Act', *Criminal Law Review*, pp. 95–116.

Clare, I., and Gudjonsson, G.H. (1992a), *Devising and Piloting a New 'Notice to Detained Persons'* (Royal Commission on Criminal Justice Research Study No. 7) (London: HMSO).

Clare, I. and Gudjonsson, G. (1992b), 'Recall and understanding of the caution and rights in police detention among persons of average intellectual ability and persons with a mild mental handicap', in M. McMurran and C. McDougall (eds), *Proceedings of the First DCLP Annual Conference* (Issues in Criminological and Legal Psychology, issue No. 17, vol. 1) (Leicester: British Psychological Society), pp. 34–42.

Clare, I.C.H., and Gudjonsson, G.H. (1993), 'Interrogative suggestibility, confabulation, and acquiescence in people with mild learning difficulties (mental handicap): Implications for reliability during police interrogation', *British Journal of Clinical Psychology*, vol. 32, pp. 295–301.

Dent, H., and Flin, R. (1992), *Children as Witnesses* (Chichester: Wiley).

Dyer, C. (1990), 'Suspects' leaflet may be reworded', *Guardian* (30 November), p. 7.

Flesch, R. (1948), 'A new readability yardstick', *Journal of Applied Psychology*, vol. 32, pp. 221–33.

Gudjonsson, G.H. (1984), 'A new scale of interrogative suggestibility', *Personality and Individual Differences*, vol. 5, pp. 303–14.

Gudjonsson, G.H. (1987), 'A parallel form of the Gudjonsson Suggestibility Scale', *British Journal of Clinical Psychology*, vol. 26, pp. 215–21.

Gudjonsson, G.H. (1990a), 'Understanding the notice to detained persons', *Law Society's Gazette*, vol. 87, No. 43, pp. 24, 27.

Gudjonsson, G.H. (1990b), 'One hundred alleged false confession cases: some normative data', *British Journal of Clinical Psychology*, vol. 29, pp. 249–30.

Gudjonsson, G.H. (1991), 'The "notice to detained persons", PACE codes, and reading ease', *Applied Cognitive Psychology*, vol. 5, pp. 89–95.

Gudjonsson, G.H. (1992a), *The Psychology of Interrogations, Confessions, and Testimony* (Chichester: Wiley).

Gudjonsson, G.H. (1992b), 'The admissibility of expert psychological and psychiatric evidence in England and Wales', *Criminal Behaviour and Mental Health*, vol. 2, pp. 245–52.

Gudjonsson, G.H. (1992c), 'Interrogation and false confessions: vulnerability factors', *British Journal of Hospital Medicine*, vol. 47, pp. 597–9.

Gudjonsson, G.H. (1993), 'Confession evidence, psychological vulnerability and expert testimony', *Journal of Community and Applied Social Psychology*, vol. 3, pp. 117–29.

Gudjonsson, G.H. (1994), 'Mental illness and "fitness" for police interview: a case study'. In preparation.

Gudjonsson, G.H., Clare, I.C.H., and Cross, P. (1992), 'The revised PACE "notice to detained persons": how easy is it to understand?', *Journal of the Forensic Science Society*, vol. 32, pp. 289–99.

Gudjonsson, G.H., Clare, I.C.H., and Rutter, S.C. (1994), 'Psychological characteristics of suspects interviewed at police stations: a factor analytic study', *Journal of Forensic Psychiatry* (in press).

Gudjonsson, G., Clare I., Rutter, S., and Pearse, J. (1993), *Persons at Risk during Interviews in Police Custody: The Identification of Vulnerabilities* (Royal Commission on Criminal Justice Research Study No. 12) (London: HMSO).

Gudjonsson, G.H. and Singh, K.K. (1984), 'The relationship between criminal conviction and interrogative suggestibility among delinquent boys', *Journal of Adolescence*, vol. 7, pp. 29–34.

Irving, B. (1980), *Police Interrogation: A Case Study of Current Practice* (Royal Commission on Criminal Procedure Research Study No. 2) (London: HMSO).

Irving, B., and McKenzie, I.K. (1989), *Police Interrogation: The Effects of the Police and Criminal Evidence Act* (London: Police Foundation).

Metropolitan Police (1991), *A Change of PACE: A Guide to the Changes to the Codes of Practice* (London: Metropolitan Police).

Mills, H. (1992a), 'Judges give evidence guidelines. Ward judgment attacks "partisan" scientists who hid damaging facts', *Independent* (5 June), p. 1.

Mills, H. (1992b), 'Ward's boast of role in IRA "not taken seriously"', *Independent on Sunday* (3 May), p. 2.

Richardson, G. (1993), *Law, Process and Custody: Prisoners and Patients* (London: Weidenfield and Nicholson).

Royal Commission on Criminal Justice (1993), *Report* (Cm 2263) (London: HMSO).

Schonell, F.J., and Goodacre, E.J. (1974), *The Psychology and Teaching of Reading*, 5th ed. (Harlow: Oliver & Boyd/Longmans).

Singh, K.K. and Gudjonsson, G.H. (1992), 'The vulnerability of adolescent boys to interrogative pressure', *Journal of Forensic Psychiatry*, vol. 3, pp. 167–70.

Spielberger, C.D. (1983), *Manual for the State-Trait Anxiety Inventory (Form Y)* (Palo Alto CA: Consulting Psychologists Press).

Spielberger, C.D., Gorsuch, R.L., and Luschene, R.E. (1970), *Manual for the State-Anxiety Inventory* (Palo Alto CA: Consulting Psychologists Press).

Wechsler, D. (1981), *WAIS-R Manual* (New York: Psychological Corporation).

7

Reflections on Current Police Practice

Tom Williamson

I have three reflections on current practice:

(a)   Unethical behaviour by interrogators has undermined public confidence and left the police service with a serious skills deficit in its ability to obtain evidence through questioning.

(b)   The principles of investigative interviewing designed to create a new approach to police questioning have not been sufficiently understood by the service.

(c)   Currently, and in particular after any removal of the right of silence, the judges will apply strict criteria before admitting evidence obtained through questioning. They will be unlikely to admit anything which is not consistent with the principles and training on investigative interviewing.

Unethical behaviour by interrogators

My first reflection is that it does not take much skill to beat a confession out of a suspect detained in police custody. The police in this country would correctly deny that such things happen but unfortunately a considerable proportion of the general public thinks that it happens regularly (e.g., Smith 1983, Jones et al. 1986, Harris Research Centre 1987).

Nor does it take much skill to fabricate a confession and allege that it was made during police questioning either in custody or on the way to the police station. A considerable proportion of the general public thinks this also happens regularly (e.g., Smith 1983, Jones et al. 1986). The lawyers' term for this is 'verballing'. Sir John Woodcock, the government's former Chief Inspector of Constabulary has called it 'noble cause' corruption (Woodcock 1992). It is also perjury, lying on oath, a criminal offence punishable with seven years' imprisonment. Former Commissioner, Sir David McNee called it 'pious perjury' (McNee 1983).

Two consequences follow from these widely held perceptions. First, if you believed that violence or verballing were sometimes or often used by the police it would be most unlikely that you would agree to any alteration to the right to silence. Secondly, not only are both of these approaches to interrogation illegal and unethical, they also deny the need for any training for police officers to improve their interviewing skills to be able to obtain evidence through questioning. Unethical behaviour, the lack of skills training and the retention of the right to silence are symptoms that within the English adversarial system of justice there has been an over-reliance on confession evidence.

The succession of cases which have been overturned by the Court of Appeal is forcing a fundamental reappraisal of the role of the investigator in an adversarial system of justice. The dangers of the investigation being too closely tied to the prosecution and conviction of suspects is gradually being realised. Within an adversarial system of justice it is only the investigator who gets close to a search for the truth. Redefining the role of the investigator as a searcher for the truth and gatherer of facts would have a very significant effect on the way investigators see themselves and conduct their interviews. It will mean that far greater effort will have to be made in obtaining better-quality statements from victims and witnesses, instead of the traditional reliance on getting a suspect to confess.

A legal framework providing safeguards for custodial questioning has gradually been built up. The problem of verballing has largely been dealt with through the introduction of tape recording of questioning in a police station. Custodial questioning is, however, inherently coercive (Irving 1980) and the recent Royal Commission on Criminal Justice (1993) considered the need for additional safeguards specifically covering 'oppressive' questioning and the questioning of suspects who were liable to make false confessions. They concluded that the arrangements under the Police and Criminal Evidence Act 1984 (PACE) and the codes of practice were fundamentally sound.

In reaching this conclusion the Royal Commission appear to have been influenced by the developments that have been taking place in police interviewing. The new approach to police interviewing was set out in Home Office Circular 22/1992. The circular laid down certain principles for investigative interviewing which were developed through collaboration between police officers, lawyers and psychologists. What was set out in the principles was in stark contrast to what the Commission found when they were sent a tape by the Lord Chief Justice after the Court of Appeal had allowed the appeal of the 'Cardiff Three', according to the Commission:

This tape contained the record of a long and highly repetitive series of questions put to one of the appellants in a loud and aggressive way. This was one of a series of tapes which recorded interviews over a prolonged period leading to damaging admissions by the suspect after his repeated denials had been ignored.

The Lord Chief Justice said:

Short of physical abuse, it is hard to conceive of a more hostile and intimidating approach by officers to a suspect.

The 'Cardiff Three' judgment has set the standard against which all future interviews will have to be assessed. The recent case of *R* v *Heron* illustrates how judges will be following the lead set by the Lord Chief Justice.

Home Office Circular 22/1992 was followed by another, 7/1993, which introduced a new training package for basic interviewing skills which we shall consider later. The circular recommended the issue of two booklets on investigative interviewing to all officers, *The Interviewer's Rule Book* and *A Guide to Interviewing*. Training courses were developed to supplement the booklets.

The principles of investigative interviewing and the new training booklets and courses were designed to provide an ethical foundation for the police in questioning suspects. They were to ensure that what was said during police questioning was said freely and recorded accurately. Officers adopting oppressive questioning styles would not only be out of step with nationally agreed guidelines on questioning but would find judges adopting a more robust position with regard to admitting confession evidence than was the case in the past. In future the judges will also be paying particular attention to confessions from those who expert psychological evidence could show were at risk in making false confessions (Gudjonsson 1992). There has to be greater awareness of these issues by police officers and also a change in questioning style in order to satisfy the legal requirement for the prosecution to show that nothing has been done which could render a confession unreliable (PACE, s. 76).

The pressure for change has built up slowly but inexorably over recent years. The transition from coercive questioning practice is only just beginning. A study by Walkley (1983) showed that over half the detectives he interviewed were prepared to use force, or the threat of force when questioning suspects. Walkley identified three types of interrogator depending on the extent to which they were prepared to go in stressing suspects. He found that 32% were prepared to use force. He called this group 'dominant'. He found a further 34%

were prepared to hint that they were willing to use force. He called this group, 'pseudo-dominant'. Another 34% were not prepared to countenance the use of force or hint that they were willing to use force. He called this group, 'non-dominant'. Walkley captures in this categorisation the idea that what separates interrogators is the degree of domineering or oppressive behaviour.

In the *Heron* case, Mr Justice Mitchell was also concerned about whether the interviewing officers had deliberately misrepresented the evidence to the suspect and said that the officers' action was, 'deliberate, to misrepresent the nature and strength of the evidence'.

During the 1980s the police service was heavily influenced by American approaches to questioning, which in turn probably reflected the lack of any suitable indigenous training material. The model of interviewing described by Inbeau et al. (1986) was particularly influential with its emphasis on persuasive questioning techniques including misrepresenting the strength of the evidence in order to get a confession.

This type of training often served to reinforce an unethical culture. Decisions by English courts have consistently nipped such practices in the bud. For example, in the case of *R v Mason* (1988) 86 Cr App R 349, the Court of Appeal held that evidence was not acceptable where an officer had lied that the suspect's fingerprints had been found. This is in stark contrast to decisions in American courts which have actively supported and legitimised a doctrine of deception as a means of gaining evidence or confessions through police questioning (Leo 1992).

Police officers would probably like to think that suspects make admissions because of skilled questioning techniques. The reality, however, is quite different. In a study of over 1,000 interviews by detectives (Moston et al. 1993) there were very few cases in which suspects were persuaded to deviate from their initial response to police questioning. Suspects who began an interview by denying their involvement were still denying it at the conclusion of questioning. The admissions which were elicited tended to be relatively spontaneous and typically occurred at an early stage of questioning.

The restrictions placed on interviewers by PACE appear to have made the detectives in this study wary of using persuasive questioning techniques.

Baldwin (1992) had access to video or audio recordings of 600 police interviews. He found that 36% of the interviews were not of an acceptable standard. He grouped his criticisms under four headings:

(a) *Ineptitude*. Officers were nervous, ill at ease and lacking in confidence.

(b) *Assumption of guilt*. Officers assumed guilt, adopted a tone of extreme scepticism, and failed to elicit any confirmatory evidence.

(c) *Poor interviewing*. Officers continually interrupted the suspect, they also had a fragile grasp of the points needed to prove an offence.

(d) *Unprofessional.* Adopting an unduly harrying and aggressive approach, and offering unfair inducements, particularly in relation to offences to be 'taken into consideration'.

The principles of investigative interviewing not understood

There was clearly a need for training. The new ethical framework on which the national training programme in investigative interviewing is based is intended to address these issues and my second reflection is that this has not been widely understood and I should therefore like to take a few minutes to discuss the principles on which investigative interviewing is based.

The first principle is intended to shift the police service from its traditional prosecution orientation and to encourage it to see its task as a search for the truth. This allows it to escape from the adversarial nature of police investigative encounters and instead adopt a more neutral position as gatherers of accurate and reliable information from suspects, witnesses or victims.

This concept of a search for the truth was picked up by the police service as the core theme of its submission to the Royal Commission on Criminal Justice. The Royal Commission were prepared to support the police service in its efforts to become better interviewers and investigators but were not prepared to alter significantly the accusatorial nature of our system of justice and make it more of an inquiry for the truth. The police may aspire to be independent seekers after the truth but they must continue to work within an accusatorial framework. All systems of justice, whether adversarial or inquisitorial have elements which are inquiries into what actually happened. In our adversarial system, the inquisitorial function is conducted only by the police. Many of the miscarriages of justice have arisen from an unduly adversarial and partisan position adopted by the police: a position which was adhered to often blindly and unreasoningly.

The second principle therefore is intended to encourage officers to approach an investigation with an open mind instead of their focus on 'interrogation' of suspects. Information obtained is to be tested against what the officer already knew or could establish. Building on the research studies, it was possible to show that a more successful approach to interviewing of suspects would be based on more thorough interviewing of victims and witnesses. It was recognised that good evidence was going to take time and this in itself was in marked contrast to the rush and expediency of contemporary interviewing practice.

The third principle is intended to encourage officers to be fair. Fortunately, this exhortation is consistent with the efforts going on within the police service following the adoption of the Statement of Common Purpose and Values. It will be seen that this places the policing task in an ethical framework:

The purpose of the police service is to uphold the law fairly and firmly, to prevent crime, to pursue and bring to justice those who break the law; to keep the Queen's Peace; to protect, help and reassure people; and to be seen to do all this with integrity, common sense and sound judgement.

We must be compassionate, courteous and patient, acting without fear or favour or prejudice to the rights of others. We need to be professional, calm and restrained in the face of violence and apply only that force which is necessary to accomplish our lawful duty.

We must strive to reduce the fears of the public and, so far as we can, to reflect their priorities in the action we take. We must respond to well founded criticism with a willingness to change.

One of Baldwin's (1992) conclusions was that senior members of the police service did not accept that there was a problem with interviewing. Police officers who have examined the spirit of PACE and the codes of practice as opposed to concentrating on parts of the text which give them most pain will see that 'fairness' is a theme which runs through it (Zander 1985). The principles of investigative interviewing are designed to help police officers in any subsequent judicial proceedings where their actions are being examined to show that they had behaved 'fairly'. If they have behaved 'fairly' but the prosecution is lost, that is a matter for those responsible for our system of criminal justice. The police service should no longer be prepared to countenance any 'noble cause' corruption. It should in future provide the officers with the necessary interviewing skills and the explicit authority to resist pressure to take expedient measures in anticipation of the justice system failing to deliver justice.

The principles contain a reference to the right to silence which continues to be a matter of concern to officers. Therefore, whilst accepting that under the law as it currently stands suspects have the right to remain silent, it was decided upon legal advice that officers were also entitled to put relevant questions to a suspect. It was accepted that there was no way in which a suspect should be forced to speak, and consequently the evidence of the police service to the Royal Commission sought a right for the prosecution and the judge to comment in cases where the right to silence had been used.

The principles are intended to convey to police officers investigating an offence that they are not required to take statements as though they were bound by the rules of evidence. What is needed is information which could be assessed and acted upon. Statements are to be a fair and accurate record of what was said, not a record which has been truncated and edited to suit the administrative convenience of the lawyers. This is to be reinforced during training with focus sessions at critical points in the investigation in order to review the information which has been collected.

Finally, the principles underline the importance of recognising the difficulties of those with special needs, including those with low IQ, learning difficulties and others who may be at risk and liable to make false confessions. A particular concern when it came to preparing the training material to support this principle is that, despite research undertaken in this area by Gudjonsson et al. (1993) for the Royal Commission on Criminal Justice, there is no agreed procedure to help interviewers identify people who may be at risk. Some training is now being given to forensic medical examiners, who are the doctors who certify whether a suspect is fit to be detained and fit to be interviewed, which may make them more effective at identifying those who are at risk. The issue of who the appropriate adult should be, what qualifications are required and where such people are to be found, is still a matter of conjecture. At this stage what is required is to make officers more aware of the reasons why some people are at risk and the initial steps they can take to address that matter prior to questioning a victim, witness or suspect.

Training materials have been developed to support the new ethical framework. A mnemonic 'PEACE' has been devised to help officers divide an interview into five discrete parts:

(a) *Preparation and planning*.

(b) Officers are trained in how to *engage* the interviewee in conversation and to explain the purpose of the interview.

(c) Officers are taught one of two methods of *allowing* the interviewee to provide an *account*. The cognitive interview is useful for obtaining excellent quality information from cooperative victims and witnesses. It can, however, be used in suspect interviews with suspects who are willing to confess and provide an account of what happened. The alternative method of 'managed conversation' can be used in interviews where the degree of cooperation is not sufficient to enable the cognitive interview to work.

(d) Officers are taught how to bring an interview to a *conclusion*.

(e) The need for an *evaluation* is taught. It is intended to create a learning culture where interviewers are continually learning from their experience. At present, despite every interview being tape-recorded, hardly anyone listens to the tape! This means that the potential for a lot of good learning is being missed.

The five-day investigative interviewing pilot courses have been evaluated (McGurk et al. 1993). The effectiveness of the course was examined by contrasting the performance of students undergoing the training with that of a control group which did not attend the course.

It was found that on a written examination of knowledge about interviewing the students performed significantly better than the controls after the course and also six months later.

113

In simulated interviews with both witnesses and suspects, the students improved significantly following the course and the improvement was maintained when tests were made six months later.

In actual interviews with suspects, there was a significant improvement in the students, and a marked superiority over the controls, following training.

Overall, students' knowledge increased and their interview skills were significantly improved. The improvement was sustained over a six-month period. The training was judged to be successful.

Stricter judicial supervision

My third reflection gives expression to a fear that the training may be delivered by officers who have previously been providing the 'persuasive questioning' type of interview training, with the result that what is actually passed on will be an attenuated form of investigative interviewing. The trainers will have learned the new words but have missed the music.

The challenge that faces the police service is therefore to ensure that the aims of investigative interviewing are carried out in practice. I will conclude with reference to three other initiatives that are intended to 'make it happen'.

Research on the management and supervision of police interviews has been undertaken (Stockdale 1993). Stockdale started from the premise that the police need mechanisms for monitoring and improving the standard of service delivery in order to meet their stated aims regarding interviews. In a study of investigataive interviewing in five forces she found that the problems which interviewers encountered were exacerbated by the fact that supervisors did not have, or did not make, time for routine supervision and monitoring. Many supervisors lacked credibility in the eyes of junior officers and the skills necessary for effective supervision and quality control of interviews. A number of potential indices of interview quality were identified and training recommendations were made. However, the study concluded that effective quality control of interviews required organisational and cultural change. A training package for supervisors will shortly be released which will contribute to cultural change.

Another project involving three participating police forces is developing a computerised interactive video training programme which will enable training in investigative interviewing to be deliverd in the workplace.

Further research is beginning into investigative interviewing needs in specialist areas.

The tools are therefore being provided to translate investigative interviewing from concept into practice. In the meantime many police interviews will be bungled, yielding little of the information which they were capable of providing, and consequently limiting the contribution which the police can make to criminal justice.

As a majority of the Royal Commission argued:

There are too many cases of improper pressure being brought to bear on suspects in police custody, even where the safeguards of PACE and the codes of practice have been supposedly in force, for the majority to regard this with equanimity.

Conclusion

In my opinion, the debate on the right to silence turns not on figures and percentages but upon public confidence in police interviewing practices (Moston et al. 1993). I strongly support the minority recommendation of the Royal Commission and also the Home Secretary's proposals to alter the right to silence. But I also support the strong stance which the courts are taking in excluding evidence obtained through oppressive questioning. Any legislative change to the right of silence is likely to be balanced by a very robust position being taken up by the judges over what they allow to go to the jury. They will do this in order to minimise the risk of any further miscarriages of justice. They are unlikely to admit anything which is not consistent with the principles and training on investigative interviewing.

References

Baldwin, J. (1992), *Video Taping Police Interviews with Suspects: An Evaluation* (Police Research Series Paper 1) (London: Home Office Police Research Group).

Gudjonsson, G. (1992), *The Psychology of Interrogations, Confessions and Testimony* (Chichester: Wiley).

Gudjonsson, G.H., Clare, I., Rutter, S., and Pearse, J. (1993), *Persons at Risk during Interviews in Police Custody: The Identification of Vulnerabilities* (Royal Commission on Criminal Justice Research Study No. 12 (London: HMSO).

Harris Research Centre (1987), *Crime in Newham: Report of a Survey of Crime and Racial Harassment in Newham* (London: Harris Research Centre for the London Borough of Newham).

Inbeau, F.E., Reid, J.E., and Buckley, J.P. (1986), *Criminal Interrogation and Confessions*, 3rd ed. (Baltimore MD: Williams & Wilkins).

Irving, B. (1980), *Police Interrogation: A Case Study of Current Practice* (Royal Commission on Criminal Procedure Research Study No. 2) (London: HMSO).

Jones, T., MacLean, M., and Young J. (1986), *The Islington Crime Survey: Crime Victimisation and Policing in Inner City London* (Aldershot: Gower).

Leo, R.A. (1992), 'From coercion to deception: the changing nature of police interrogation in America', *Crime, Law and Social Change*, vol. 18, pp. 35–9.

McGurk, B., Carr, M., and McGurk, D. (1993), *Investigative Interviewing Courses for Police Officers: An Evaluation* (Police Research Series Paper 4) (London: Home Office).

McNee, Sir David (1983), *McNee's Law: The Memoirs of Sir David McNee: Five Critical Years at the Metropolitan Police* (London: Collins).

Moston, S., Stephenson, G.M., and Williamson, T.M. (1993), 'The incidence, antecedents and consequences of the use of right of silence during police questioning', *Criminal Behaviour and Mental Health*, vol. 3, pp. 30–47.

Royal Commission on Criminal Justice (1993), *Report* (Cm 2263) (London: HMSO).

Smith, D.J. (1983), *Police and People in London I: A Survey of Londoners* (London: Policy Studies Institute).

Smith, D.J., and Gray, J. (1983), *Police and People in London IV: The Police in Action* (London: Policy Studies Institute).

Stockdale, J. (1993), *Management and Supervision of Police Interviews* (Police Research Series Paper 5) (London: Home Office).

Walkley, J. (1983), *Police Interrogation: A Study of the Psychology, Theory and Practice of Police Interrogations and the Implications for Police Training*. MSc thesis, Cranfield Institute of Technology.

Woodcock, Sir John (1992), 'Trust in the Police — The Search for Truth'. Address to the International Police Exhibition and Conference, 13 October 1992, London.

Zander, M. (1985), *The Police and Criminal Evidence Act 1984* (London: Sweet & Maxwell).

8

Bias and Suggestibility: Is There an Alternative to the Right to Silence?

A.A.S. Zuckerman

Introduction

The criminal trial system is regarded as standing at the pinnacle of the State's machinery for dealing with crime. But the courts deal with only a small proportion of crimes committed.[1] Their function is more indirect: to express societal disapproval through a public and somewhat theatrical show. This is not to denigrate the role of the courts or dismiss it as futile. The criminal trial does have important functions in the development of norms for criminal responsibility and in fostering respect for the law. But its success in this regard hinges on the extent to which it is perceived as a just and effective method for dealing with those charged with crime. Only if the public can be persuaded that verdicts conform to the factual truth and that they are arrived at by a fair procedure will the public be prepared to accept those verdicts at face value.

That public confidence has been seriously undermined by recent exposure of miscarriage of justice goes without saying. Not only has police evidence been shown to be unreliable but the court procedures themselves have been shown to be inept in providing adequate protection to the innocent, and the appeal courts have been shown to be unable to put right that which has gone wrong at first instance. As a result, a Royal Commission was set up 'to examine the effectiveness of the criminal justice system ... in securing the conviction

---

[1] In England there are about 8.2 million offences per year; of which 3.34 million are reported and 2.1 million are recorded; of which only 0.55 million are actually cleared up. Only 1.6% of all crimes are dealt with by the courts, of which the great majority involve no trial at all since they end in guilty pleas and a bargained sentence.

of those guilty of criminal offences and the acquittal of those who are innocent, having regard to the efficient use of resources' (Royal Commission on Criminal Justice 1993).

The purpose of this chapter is to identify the flaw in the strategy embraced by the Royal Commission for dealing with the problem of miscarriage of justice. It will be argued that the roots of miscarriage of justice almost invariably lie in the police investigation. The Royal Commission, it is maintained, have therefore been ill advised to devote so much of their efforts to legal aspects, particularly those affecting post-investigatory procedures, and relatively little attention to the need to improve the investigatory process. The principal reason for this lopsided approach lies in the Commission's policy not to question the existing structure of the criminal justice system and instead concentrate their efforts on seeking improvement in its present mode of operation.

While most of the Commission's suggestions are sensible, they are unlikely to provide an effective cure to the deeper causes of miscarriage of justice. No improvement in the trial system can alter the fact that the trial is not an entirely effective instrument for determining the reliability of the police case, which is presented by the prosecution. The main cause of miscarriage of justice, errors made during the police investigation, are often too deeply buried to be capable of being detected at the trial. Yet the treatment of the causes of these errors in the Royal Commission's report is, at best, half-hearted. The Commission provided a superficial account of the sources of police errors and made weak recommendations for their eradication. Indeed, it may be said that the most important lesson to be derived from this report is that we have gone almost as far as we can with addressing the problem of miscarriage of justice under the present structure of criminal investigations.

It will be argued that there is little hope of a substantial improvement unless we are prepared to find ways to overcome the underlying problems in police investigations. These consist in police bias and in the suggestibility of suspects and witnesses. A proposal for a cooperative investigatory process is put forward which entails a gradual, progressive and mutual exchange of information between the suspect and his or her legal representatives, on the one hand, and the police on the other. This proposal has implications for the right to silence and a comment is made about its curtailment.

The dependence of the trial process on police investigation

The existing strategy may be described as top-heavy. The most important stage is regarded to be the public trial. To this stage is assigned not only the great moral virtue of justice seen to be done but also the prowess of divination of fact. The verdict of the jury, of 12 persons fair and true, underwritten, when desired, with the appeal judges' seal of approval, is regarded not only as a fair and proper arbiter of guilt or innocence but also as a factually accurate one. The philosophy underlying the criminal justice system holds that judge and the jury can discriminate between true and false testimony, between reliable and unreliable police evidence, between well-supported inferences and poorly supported ones. Although judges and the juries do not themselves investigate the facts alleged by the prosecution, they are presumed to have the capacity of turning the evidence presented to them into a veritable account of the events as they really took place.

One of the misconceptions lurking behind this view is that prosecution evidence consists purely of raw facts. These facts, so the assumption goes, are presented to the trier of fact whose role is to draw from them correct inferences regarding the accused's guilt. Yet the most cursory examination will reveal that the case for the prosecution does not consist purely of elemental pieces of reality; a fingerprint, a bullet, a corpse or a witness account of such elements. The police construct and present an entire picture of reality which is interlaced with evaluative conclusions (such as the description of the conduct to fit a particular legal definition), with evidence created by the police in its interaction with the suspect (the confession), and is shaped by numerous decisions, mostly unrecorded and sometimes even unconscious, to pursue certain leads or hypotheses and drop others, to ask certain questions rather than others, and to look in some places but not in others. As the Royal Commission observed:

> Few people would nowadays regard the role of the police as being confined to arrest and questioning leading to a charge. The police are plainly involved in preparing the case for prosecution after charge. (Royal Commission on Criminal Justice 1993, p. 17.)

The task that the trier of fact has to fulfil does not involve so much the drawing of inferences from relevant evidence as the testing for reliability and verisimilitude of an entire account of past events. This makes the trier of fact's job tricky due to the combined effect of two factors. First, it is practically impossible to scrutinise all the aspects of the case for the prosecution. Before trial, the defence have neither the powers nor the resources to subject to close scrutiny the police investigation and the exact course that it followed, nor are the defence in a position to mount a parallel investigation of their own. At the trial, the defence are limited to examining the product of the police investigation which, as we have already observed, is not simply a collection of facts. Behind the facade of the facts presented at the trial lie a whole host of value judgments, policy decisions and cognitive conceptions of reality, most of which can no longer be unravelled in the aftermath of an investigation.

These limitations upon the defence and, inevitably, upon the trial process are aggravated by a second factor: the presumption of police integrity. By and large jurors and judges take at face value the integrity of the police and the prosecution. Except at periods of exceptional mistrust of the police, such as may be the situation at present, it is understandable that the integrity of the law enforcement agencies should be accepted and respected. The assumption of integrity is of course not absolute, but it is sufficiently well-rooted to form a potent piece of background information. While the assumption of police integrity is widespread, if not evenly distributed, it is particularly strongly held by prosecuting authorities and the judiciary, due to the institutional reliance that these authorities place on the police. The assumption of police integrity tends to gather momentum as prosecuting authorities commit themselves to the version of events constructed by the police.

If we bear in mind that at the criminal trial the assumption of police integrity combines with the impracticability of dissecting the police investigation in its entirety, it is easy to understand why the trial process is not an entirely satisfactory method of determining the truth of the case for the prosecution. Yet, even if it were possible for the trier of fact to subject the case for the prosecution to rigorous and comprehensive examination, we would still be justified in asking whether it is sensible to direct most of the effort in divising the best possible trial procedure for gauging the reliability of the police and prosecution case. Should we not place at least as much importance on the quality of the police investigation from which the case for the prosecution emerges?

Given the extent to which the criminal trial relies on police investigations and their findings and given the limited extent to which these can be probed, it seems reasonable to focus the efforts of reform on the initial investigative stage of the criminal process. Indeed, experience shows that miscarriage of justice almost invariably has its root in faulty police work. Most commonly, it is an unreliable confession, or a false piece of forensic evidence or a misdirected police inquiry which is found at the root of convictions of innocent persons. It follows that a substantial improvement in the quality of guilty verdicts can be achieved only by a commensurate improvement in the reliability of the results obtained by police investigations. To obtain such an improvement we must first identify the factors which tend to render the results of police investigations unreliable.

Failure of the Royal Commission to address the problems of police investigations

Methodological obstacles faced by police investigators

It is widely believed, by both the police and the general public, that the predominant, if not the only, problem encountered in the investigation of crime lies in the obstructive habits of criminals and their lack of cooperation in getting themselves apprehended and convicted. Indeed, this assumption has now led to the curtailment of the right to silence (see below). It is of course true that criminals are evasive, but this is as much the main problem in the investigation of crime as is the elusiveness of the cause of cancer in cancer research. We have to take it for granted that criminals go to great lengths to evade detection and punishment, just as we acknowledge that it is hard to identify the cause of cancer. Once this is accepted, attention can then turn to the need to devise suitable tools for the task in hand. The problem encountered in the investigation of crime lies in the difficulty of devising a methodology which will yield reliable evidence about the commission of crimes, just as the problem in cancer research lies in the difficulty of devising experiments that will isolate the cause for cancer. Notwithstanding the triteness of this observation, the methodological problems involved in the investigation of crime have gone largely unacknowledged.

The methodology of crime investigation is bedevilled by two principal obstacles that have long been recognised in scientific investigation: bias and artefact (Zuckerman 1992). It is well documented that investigators in science tend to be biased in favour of their own hypotheses. Bias can have several results: interpreter effect, observer effect, and intentional effect. An experimenter who approaches an experiment with a belief that his or her hypothesis will be borne out by the experiment tends to make mistakes of interpretation that favour the hypothesis and tends to overlook interpretations which are unfavourable to it. Further, belief in one's hypothesis has been found to lead to errors in observing and in recording the results of experiments. Lastly, even scientists have been known to cheat. Like policemen, scientists are under pressure to produce results and competition amongst them can be intense, with the result that some scientists have been known to take short cuts.

To make things worse, bias is joined by a further distorting factor, known in science as artefact or suggestibility. This factor is responsible for distortions in the response of the subjects of investigations. Both animals and humans seem to be prone to them. In experiments on rats it has been shown that where experiments predicted the rats to be maze-bright, the rats lived up to their expectations. Similarly, where the rats were expected to be maze-dull the rats

121

also fulfilled expectations (Zuckerman 1992). The reason was that experimenters who believed their subjects to be brighter behaved differently towards the rats and thus affected the rats' learning abilities. Similar effects have been detected in human subjects, where subjects have shown a marked and consistent tendency to fulfil whatever expectation the experimenter may harbour. The distorting factor may consist in the communication to the subject of the experimenter's expectation, which expectation causes the subject to respond in a way that would satisfy the expectation. Expectancy has been proved to be communicated to the subject immediately on first contact with the experimenter. It is communicated unconsciously by both auditory and visual cues. This accounts for the fact that even when experimenters are aware of the expectancy factor, its effect can persist.

These two distorting factors present a major obstacle to attaining reliable objectivity in the results of police investigations. We hardly need empirical research be persuaded of the presence of bias and suggestibility in police investigations. The police interrogator tends to approach his or her suspect, and sometimes even ordinary witnesses, with definite expectations which could inadvertently affect the information obtained from them. Quite probably, expectancy effects were behind the otherwise inexplicable phenomenon of misidentification of the same suspect by a number of independent witnesses. We know that police bias, and on occasion bias by forensic scientists, played a dominant role in recent cases of miscarriage of justice in England.

The Royal Commission's neglect of methodological obstacles

Although the factors of bias and suggestibility have been known for nearly a century, little interest has been shown by those engaged in the administration of criminal justice, including the legal profession, in studying their effects on criminal investigations. Until 1985 police interrogation of suspects, the mainstay of the case for the prosecution in a large proportion of cases, was left entirely to the discretion of police officers who were as ignorant of bias and artefact as they were reluctant to concede any monitoring of their practices. The Police and Criminal Evidence Act 1984, which was enacted in the wake of the report of the Royal Commission on Criminal Procedure (1981), brought about a significant change in this respect for it introduced greater transparency into police practices. It was followed by the implementation of novel practices of monitoring the treatment of suspects while in custody and of recording interviews with them. The 1993 Royal Commission Report builds upon this earlier report and recommends further improvements.

At the outset of their discussion on the process of police investigation the Royal Commission on Criminal Justice acknowledged that the 'manner in which police investigations are conducted is of critical importance to the functioning of the criminal justice system' (1993, p. 9). Yet having accepted that much depends on police investigations, the methodology of police investigation is passed over with striking superficiality. The Commission drew attention to the tendency of police officers to approach interviews with suspects with an assumption of the suspect's guilt and an expectation of being able to obtain a confession. The initial assumption of the investigator, the Commission observed, makes it difficult for the investigator to keep an open mind. The Commission warned against the deleterious effects of oppressive questioning and of suggestibility and about the importance of curtailing the length of interviews and affording suspects adequate rest (1993, pp. 13–14).

However, having identified some sources of error, the Commission did little by way of discussing how to counteract error. The Commission thought that all that was necessary to put matters right was for officers to be trained 'to recognise these dangers and in particular to recognise the need to listen to what the suspect says and ... to follow up and check on his or her story' (1993, pp. 12–13). To achieve this goal, the Commission seemed to think (1993, p. 13), police officers need do no more than observe the following guidelines, which have recently been laid down in a Home Office Circular as follows:

(a)   The role of investigative interviewing is to obtain accurate and reliable information from suspects, witnesses or victims in order to discover the truth about matters under police investigation.

(b)   Investigative interviewing should be approached with an open mind. Information obtained from the person who is being interviewed should always be tested against what the interviewing officer already knows or what can reasonably be established.

(c)   When questioning anyone a police officer must act fairly in the circumstances of each individual case.

(d)   The police interviewer is not bound to accept the first answer given. Questioning is not unfair merely because it is persistent.

(e)   Even when the right of silence is exercised by a suspect, the police still have a right to put questions.

(f)   When conducting an interview, police officers are free to ask questions in order to establish the truth; except for interviews with child victims of sexual or violent abuse which are to be used in criminal proceedings, they are not constrained by the rules applied to lawyers in court.

(g)   Vulnerable people, whether victims, witnesses, or suspects, must be treated with particular consideration at all times.

These guidelines are so general that some of them would obtain in respect of the investigation of fact in many other fields. For is it not the role of every social scientist, industrial planner, market researcher or social worker to 'obtain accurate and reliable evidence', or to approach interviewing 'with an open mind'? What the Commission did not discuss is why it is so difficult to keep an open mind and to obtain reliable evidence and by what methods these obstacles may be overcome.

It seems that the Commission did little more than utter the usual homilies about the importance of training police investigators, of supervising their work, and of the need for adequate scientific and logistic aids (1993, p. 9). The police are exhorted not to jump too quickly to conclusions and not to press too early for a confession but, instead, to first gather all the relevant evidence, including exculpatory evidence (1993, p. 10). However, welcome as these pieces of advice are, they are unlikely to bear fruit unless proper methods are devised for maintaining objectivity in investigation. Even in science, experimenters do not rely on good will in order to keep an open mind. Rather, they employ methods which insulate experiments from the experimenter's prejudices and expectations.

In chapter 7, Tom Williamson draws attention to efforts made by the police to learn from research studies that have drawn attention to the dangers inherent in custodial questioning. These efforts are laudable and it is hoped that they would bear fruit. But it is not unrealistic to think that such attempts would have been more widespread and better directed if they had received adequate conceptual impetus from the Royal Commission report.

Confusion of the factual and the normative in the report

As things stand, the fault of generality in the Royal Commission's report (1993) is as nothing when compared to the more serious defect of confusion of objectives, with which the report is suffused. As panoramic as the first two of the above guidelines may be, they at least deal with cognitive aspects of factual investigation. The remaining guidelines have little to do with cognition and are therefore irrelevant to factual errors. Rather, they are concerned with the idea of procedural fairness, with whether persistent questioning is fair, or whether questioning is fair after the suspect has asserted his or her constitutional right to say nothing. It is not suggested that the concern with fairness is misplaced in the context of police investigation. On the contrary, procedural fairness is as vital to this stage of the criminal process as it is at the trial. What is, however, maintained is that when devising a strategy for the conduct of police investigation it is necessary to be quite clear about the distinction between cognitive or factual aspects, i.e., factors that help or hinder the determination of truth, on the one hand, and independent legal or moral standards, such as the constitutional right against self-incrimination, on the other hand.

In this regard the Royal Commission have followed the general tendency of criminal procedure scholarship of giving prominence to legal standards and overlooking cognitive aspects. The preoccupation with fairness has often overshadowed the need to devise methods for gathering and interpreting evidence which are capable of yielding reliable data. The Royal Commission seemed to believe that the notion of fairness could do the work which, in a rational framework, should be carried out by devices designed to overcome the cognitive factors which obstruct factual reliability in police investigations.

A further familiar plank which is commonly used to strengthen the reliability of police investigations is police discipline. Again, no one would dispute the importance of discipline. A poorly motivated, inadequately paid, and ill-supervised police force might do a lot of harm. Adherence to norms of civilised treatment, conformity with high standards of integrity in the treatment of suspects, and respect for constitutional rights are important objectives. Yet it is crucial to appreciate how far discipline, in this sense, can underwrite the reliability of the case prepared by the police. Conformity with basic standards of decent treatment and of integrity can reduce the cruder types of manipulation of suspects. Tighter supervision of investigators and closer observance of the codes of practice would prevent some of the more extreme forms of corner cutting. Suggestions such as issuing officers with notebooks containing fixed and numbered pages (Royal Commission on Criminal Justice 1993, p. 22) would doubtless make it more difficult for investigators to alter their contemporaneous accounts later. Yet these measures do not and cannot significantly reduce the effects of bias and suggestibility.

Much the same thing can be said about the Royal Commission's contribution to the treatment of suspects. Most of their recommendations are sensible. It is suggested that a confession made by a suspect outside the police station should be put to the suspect at the beginning of the taped interview in the station and that the suspect should be invited to comment on it (Royal Commission on Criminal Justice 1993, p. 28). If the suspect repudiates the confession then the trial judge would have a discretion whether to admit it in evidence or exclude it (ibid., pp. 60–1). It is suggested that video cameras should be installed in the custody office, where the detention of suspects is reviewed by custody officers, and in the passages leading to the cells (ibid., p. 33). One of the most telling passages in the report deals with the video recording of interviews. The Commission had the advantage of looking at experimental projects in which suspects' interviews were recorded on a video tape. They noted the vividness of the records and their immediacy, but also went on to draw attention to the prejudice that the showing of such tapes may produce in juries and magistrates:

> Suspects will seldom be at their best in the police station, especially if they have just been arrested and are in a state of semi-shock ... It is all too easy even for trained observers to mistake small gestures and tricks of demeanour for symptoms of guilt when they may be symptoms only of nervousness or anxiety. What is more, visual impact is so powerful and immediate that it may have the effect of distracting the viewer from what is actually said. (Ibid., p. 40.)

These considerations led the Commission to reject the showing of video recordings to juries. Instead they recommended the retention of audio recordings at the trial, but they also sought to encourage research into video recording with view to determining the force of the anxiety expressed in the paragraph just quoted.

It is quite extraordinary that in one and the same breath the Royal Commission should both correctly identify matters which may distort a police interrogation and at the same time assume that only triers of fact are at risk of being affected by them but not the police. Research in psychology shows that prejudicial effects can be as powerful, and possibly more so, on those immediately involved in the interview. Police officers may just as easily mistake general nervousness or fear for consciousness of guilt. Indeed, officers may attach exaggerated importance to such indicators as a result of their preconceived assumption that the suspect they interview is guilty; for to be arrested, even only for the purpose of questioning, the police have to have a reasonable suspicion. Further, the interrogator will not unreasonably assume that a suspect who is indeed guilty would tend to lie about his or her complicity, with the result that denials may strengthen the investigator's suspicion rather than reduce it.

Perhaps the Royal Commission thought that police investigators are less susceptible to mistakes of this kind because experience will have taught them to discriminate between true and false indicators of guilt. There is, however, no evidence for such supposition. Indeed, research into interviewing techniques suggests otherwise. Such research also shows that subjects are liable to be influenced by the demeanour and assumptions of the investigator and that no amount of experience can reduce these effects (Rosenthal 1969). Perhaps the Royal Commission thought that, unlike juries, the police have the facility of examining the impressions that they obtain from interviews with suspects in the light of other evidence and that, unlike juries, they are better able to overcome any prejudice that the interview has created in their minds. Again, there is little evidence to suggest that this is so. Indeed, such evidence as exists about the effects of bias generally shows that bias leads the investigator to seek evidence that supports his or her hypothesis and to overlook evidence that contradicts it. Perhaps the Commission thought that by keeping the video recording away from juries, any prejudice will remain confined to the investigation. However, as we have observed, once created in the investigator's mind, prejudice can permeate the results on the investigation.

By banning video-taped interviews from the courts the Royal Commission have followed a strategy of distancing the trier of fact from the primary sources which may create prejudice, but overlooked their prejudicial effects on the investigation as a whole and on the case that is constructed by the police and the prosecution. Indeed, it may be argued that, far from protecting accused persons from prejudice, such a strategy may increase the prejudicial effects. For it would tend to create the impression that the evidence presented at the trial is clear of bias, whereas in reality bias was not eradicated from the choice of evidence, whether testimonial or circumstantial, nor from the way in which interviews with suspects and witnesses were conducted.

The flaws in the treatment of confessions and the right to silence

The treatment of confessions by the Royal Commission discloses a similar blend of awareness of the risks combined with an inability to depart from entrenched procedures. The Commission identified a number of factors that may lead to false confessions. Prominent amongst them are the desire to obtain an immediate advantage, such as release from detention, suggestibility, and downright falsification by unscrupulous police officers (Royal Commission on Criminal Justice 1993, pp. 57, 60). It was suggested to the Commission that a rule that only tape-recorded confessions would be admissible in evidence might help to overcome these distorting factors. The Commission rejected this proposal noting that the fact that a confession was recorded was no guarantee of its truth, and that such a rule would result in the loss of genuine confessions made outside the police station, when recording was impossible or impractical (1993, pp. 60–1). The Commission also considered a proposal that a confession should not be admissible at the trial unless obtained in the presence of a solicitor. In support of this proposal it had been pointed out, amongst others, that the presence of a solicitor would help ensure that the interview was conducted fairly and would reduce the pressure and anxiety felt by the suspect. Rejecting this proposal the Commission noted that the solicitor's presence at the interview would not necessarily prevent pressure from being placed on the suspect before the interview and, further, that the quality of solicitors was often such that their presence at the interview could not be relied upon to prevent anxiety or pressure or unfairness (1993, pp. 61–2).

The Commission were, of course, right in thinking that tape recording does not warrant truth and that a solicitor's presence does not necessarily eradicate pressure and anxiety. But this realisation should have at least led to a train of inquiry as to how the distorting effects of interrogation might be overcome. Instead, the Commission placed faith in the ability of prosecutors and triers of fact to identify, upon hearing a recorded confession, any signs of oppression or other distorting factors, such as nervousness, which might undermine the reliability of confessions. Having adverted earlier to the prejudicial effect that a video-recorded confession might have on the trier of fact, the Commission's faith seems to be misplaced. For it is improbable that prejudice is eradicated by simply removing the visual aspect of the interview and offering the trier of fact only the auditory one.

An interesting light on the Commission's thinking is thrown by their treatment of the right to silence. The Commission were pressed with a suggestion that adverse comment should be allowed at the trial upon a suspect's refusal to answer police questions. A majority of the Commission rejected this view on the grounds that there was a substantial 'risk that the extra pressure on suspects to talk in the police station and the adverse inference invited if they do not may result in more convictions of the innocent' (1993, p. 54). The Commission also noted (1993, pp. 52–3) that only a small proportion of all suspects exercise their right to silence (between 6 and 10% outside London and between 14 and 16% in London). The juxtaposition of the Commission's conclusion and the statistical data prompts the following question: If nearly 90% of suspects make a statement, is it reasonable to suppose that they all do so without any pressure from the police? And, if police pressure can render a confession unreliable, is it not reasonable to suppose that a proportion of the confessions obtained are unreliable? In other words, should we not worry about the reliability of those confessions too, in the same way that we are concerned about the reliability of confessions obtained by threat of an adverse comment? Perhaps conscious of these questions the Royal Commission observed (1993, p. 64) that:

> Research has conclusively demonstrated that under certain circumstances individuals may confess to crimes they have not committed and that it is more likely that they will do so in interviews conducted in police custody even when proper safeguards apply....
>
> Further, even proper pressure may lead to a false confession. Once a confession has been obtained the likely consequence is that the investigation will come to an end.

The Commission might have added that even if the investigation does not come to an end upon the obtaining of a confession, the presence of a confession will tend to strengthen the investigator's assumption of the suspect's guilt and the investigator's tendency to seek incriminating evidence and overlook exculpatory indications.

As in a number of other contexts the Commission's awareness of the inherent difficulties in obtaining reliable evidence by interrogation did not inspire them to seek ways of overcoming the underlying difficulty. This is not surprising given their pursuit of the traditional strategy of placing one's faith in the trial and believing that if only the police were a disciplined and trustworthy organisation, the trier of fact would be able to sort out truth from falsehood.

Defence and police interaction during the pre-trial stages

Recommendations regarding defence disclosure

Most of the Commission's efforts were devoted to seeking improvements in the post investigative legal procedures. Every stage of the process comes under review: the prosecution, pre-trial procedure, the trial, the appeal process and post-appeal procedure for the correction of miscarriage of justice. Of the 187 pages of the report, fewer than a third are concerned with the police stage. The Commission recommended closer cooperation between the police and the prosecution. They sought improvement in the pre-trial proceedings, such as the introduction of preparatory pre-trial hearings. They discussed the rules of evidence and jury selection. They dealt with the provision of forensic services and considered the appeal mechanism. Most of this is not pertinent to our immediate concern, but the Commission's treatment of advance disclosure by the defence is of interest as it throws light on an important aspect of the criminal process: the interaction between the accused and his or her accusers.

The Commission attached considerable importance to improving the process of preparation for trial. Its starting-point was that 'Crown court trials can only proceed on the basis of full disclosure by the prosecution of all the evidence in its possesion that is relevant to the case' (1993, p. 91). In England the proecution are under an obligation to disclose to the defence material in their possession which is relevant to the case. This enables the defence to prepare their case, but no comparable obligation of disclosure rests on the defence. The Commission set out the present position (1993, p. 97):

Although ... the obligations on the prosecution to disclose their case are extensive, the duty of the defence to reciprocate is limited. Defendants may, without risking adverse comment, decline to cooperate in any way and at any stage of the criminal proceedings against them except where they are intending to call alibi evidence. They need do no more than deny the offence and register a plea of not guilty. If the defence takes this course, the

129

prosecution will lead its evidence at the trial and the defence, after testing the prosecution case in cross-examination to whatever extent is felt appropriate, will invite the jury to conclude that the prosecution has failed to make out their case.

The Commission proposed a radical departure from this one-sided principle (1993, p. 97):

> With one dissident, we believe that there are powerful reasons for extending the obligations on the defence to provide advance disclosure. If all the parties had in advance an indiction of what the defence would be, this would not only encourage earlier and better preparation of cases but might well result in the prosecution being dropped in the light of the defence disclosure, an earlier resolution through a plea of guilty, or the fixing of an earlier trial date. The length of the trial would also be more readily estimated, leading to a better use of the time both of the court and of those involved in the trial; and there would be kept to a minimum those cases where the defendant withholds his or her defence until the last possible moment in the hope of confusing the jury or evading investigation of a fabricated defence.

Under the Commission's proposals (1993, p. 99), the defence would be required to reveal the substance of their case before trial or indicate that they would not be calling evidence but will simply argue that the prosecution have failed to make out their case. Where a defendant puts forward at the trial a defence without having given prior notice, or where a different defence from that notified is put forward or where mutually inconsistent defences are notified, the prosecution would be allowed, with leave of the judge, to comment on the matter, and the judge could also comment when summing up (ibid., pp. 99–100). To limit the impact of the procedural advantage that the prosecution might gain from the Commission's proposal, the Commission suggested that a disclosed defence should not be revealed to the jury as part of the case for the prosecution, but should be commented upon only once that defence, or an alternative defence has been advanced at the trial.

Flawed mutuality in the Commission's recommendations

The Commission were right to suppose that the ability of the prosecution to withstand a challenge to their case is influenced by the extent to which they receive advance notice of the defence's case. Advance notice is, after all, a requisite of procedural fairness. But the promotion of mutuality at the trial immediately raises the question of mutuality during police investigation. For if the prosecution are to have the same procedural advantage as the defence at the trial, should not the suspect have the same procedural advantage as the police during the investigation? Sadly, the Royal Commission did not consider this question.

They did make, however, some observations which are pertinent to these matters. In reaching their conclusion favouring defence disclosure the Commission adverted to the argument that the proposal goes counter to the privilege against self-incrimination. However, they disposed of this objection by saying (1993, pp. 97–8) that where:

> defendants advance a defence at the trial it does not amount to an infringement of their privilege not to incriminate themselves if advance warning of the substance of such a defence has to be given. The matter is simply one of timing. We emphasise that under our proposal defendants may, if they so choose, still stay silent throughout the trial.

This view has implications for the question whether suspects should be required to mention to the police their refutation of the allegations against them.

The Commission had been pressed, as we have already observed, with a suggestion that the suspect's right to silence be modified so that instead of being warned that he or she need say nothing during interrogation a suspect would be told, 'You have a right to remain silent but if you fail to answer a relevant question or to mention a fact which you later rely on in any trial, a court or jury may conclude that your silence supports the evidence against you'. The reasoning the Commission employed in advocating pre-trial disclosure by the defence would also apply here. It may similarly be said that a requirement to disclose information in the police station does not give rise to a question of principle but is simply a matter of timing, because a suspect is merely asked to disclose only such information as would have to be disclosed at the trial, if a defence is to be put forward. Indeed, it may be said that the police station is the appropriate place for investigating the suspect's explanations. For if the defence is disclosed only after the police investigation and during preparation for the trial, the police investigation will have ended by then and many of the investigatory tools for testing the suspect's explanations will have lapsed.

While the Commission overlooked this aspect of mutuality, it did express a view on another aspect: the provision of information to the suspect during interrogation. The Commission sought improvements in the opportunity of suspects to obtain legal advice, in the provision of information by the police to legal advisers in order to enable them to advise suspects adequately, and in the quality of the legal advice on offer to suspects (1993, pp. 35–9). They recommended that solicitors attending suspects in custody should be given a copy of the custody record, which contains information of the suspect's custody history. In the following two paragraphs the Commission set out their views of the relationship between the police and the suspect's legal adviser (1993, p. 36):

> We ... recommend that ... solicitors should be able to hear the tapes of any interviews which may have taken place with their clients before the solicitor's arrival at the police station ... Solicitors should also be given a copy of the tape as soon as practicable after charge.
>
> The police should see it as their duty to enable solicitors to advise their clients on the basis of the fullest appropriate information. We appreciate that not all the information can be released in all cases. But if no information is given to the solicitor and the suspect is confused or unclear, as sometimes happens, about what he or she is supposed to have done, then the solicitor may have little choice but to advise the suspect to say nothing in answer to police questions. It is therefore in the interests of the police to make available such information as they can in the interests of innocent suspects if it helps them to clear the matter up more quickly. We therefore recommend that Code C be amended so as to encourage the police to inform the suspect's solicitor of at least the genearl nature of the case and the prima facie evidence against the suspect.

Given the truism that it is in the interest of suspects who are confused, or inarticulate, to maintain silence, one would have expected the Royal Commission not to confine its discussion to the provision of information to solicitors. Such limitation leaves out of view the vulnerabiity of unrepresented suspects, who form the majority of suspects. The figures provided to the Commission suggest that some two thirds of suspects do not ask to see a solicitor.[2]

The unfairness of questioning a suspect who is kept in the dark about the case and the evidence that the police have can be serious and the risk of distortion considerable. It has been observed earlier that the case constructed by the police is not made up of elementary facts or pieces of information that are present in the world of fact independently of police activities. The interview with the suspect does not only elicit information which has been in the suspect's mind. The interrogation is an interactive process in which the participants respond to, and influence, each other. The interrogator would tend to approach the interrogation with a belief in the suspect's guilt. An experienced and competent police interrogator will try to elicit from the suspect answers that fit his or her hypothesis and will try to construct a damning case so as to fit the response

---

[2] In 32% of the cases looked at suspects asked for legal advice, and received it in 29% before being interviewed. The proportions were much higher in a Crown Court study: 66% and 53% respectively; see Royal Commission on Criminal Justice 1993, p. 35.

obtained from the suspect. If the suspect is kept unaware of the case against him or her, the interrogation is an entirely one-sided process in which the suspect is used as a passive subject around which the police weave the fabric of the damning case.

The provision of information to the suspect's solicitor could enable the solicitor to improve the suspect's position in the interrogation by making it less one-sided. If the solicitor knows what the factual allegations are and how they are supported, he or she could ensure that the suspect's interrogation is not manipulated to fit the police's theory rather than test the suspect's account. At the very least the solicitor would be able to insist that the interrogation is confined to those allegations for which the police have some supporting evidence, or that the questioning is limited to the offence and its immediate circumstances.

However, as with other aspects of the investigatory stage, the Royal Commission contented themselves with a superficial discussion and failed to explore the deep implications of their own observations about defence involvement in the investigatory stage.

Levelling the field of police interrogation

The remaining portion of this chapter will examine the potential for improving the suspect's protection in the police station by greater involvement of the defence in the investigatory process.

Such involvement has the potential of offering a way of combating unreliability in the police case. The participation of the suspect's solicitor at some stage of the investigation might provide a counterbalance to the distorting factors of bias and suggestibility, by requiring the police to meet objections and face the possibiity that other points of view might be viable and that further lines of inquiry might be called for. In other words, the quality of that police case might be enhanced by exposing it to scrutiny and challenge from the suspect's solicitor.

The problem of mutual suspicion

The implementation of such a scheme would, however, have to overcome some major problems, the most obvious of which is the mutual suspicion and adversity between the suspect and the police. Mutual suspicion in this situation is understandable. The police are not unreasonable to fear that a guilty suspect will tend to tailor his or her replies to meet the evidence that the police hold or, knowing what the police have, take great care not to enlighten them on what they do not know; not to mention the possibility that the suspect, or his or her associates, would tamper with evidence and witnesses. And, by the same token, defence lawyers are not unreasonable in fearing that if they reveal their defence, the police would seek ways of neutralising any exculpatory factors.

However, this mistrust need not constitute an insurmountable obstacle. Adversity, hostility, suspicion and diametrically opposed aims are not features which are unique to criminal investigations. They are present in the commercial world, and in national and international politics. The key to a successful cooperative process in a hostile environment is that at no stage must any of the participants feel excessively exposed compared with other participants. This state of affairs may be achieved by a process of interchange, or negotiation, in which the exposure, the give and take, are gradual, progressive and mutual.

Gradual, progressive and mutual exchange of information

At present, the suspect must either submit to an open-ended interrogation, without being given any information in advance, or, alternatively, withhold cooperation altogether, thus forgoing the chance of persuading the police to desist from pursuing the investigation against him or her. It should be possible to construct a more flexible and balanced procedure. For example, the extent of the suspect's questioning could be in proportion to the information revealed to the suspect about the incriminating evidence against him or her. If, at the start of the investigation, the police are not ready to tell the suspect all they have got against him or her, the interview could be limited to questions of which the suspect has been notified in advance and on which he or she has been able to consult with a lawyer. Thus the police would be able to obtain some information, but they would not be entitled to probe all that the suspect knows, and they would not be able to cross-examine the suspect and test his or her reactions. Such a constraint on the police in obtaining the suspect's agreement to free-ranging questioning may lead the police to prefer to put off a fully fledged interrogation until they have done everything possible to secure the investigation and tie up any loose ends. But this may be no bad thing.

The kind of gradual process of exchange of information described above would culminate at the stage at which the defence have access to information about all the steps that have been taken and materials that have been obtained during the investigation; excluding, perhaps, secret operational details. At that stage it would be for the defence to comment on any weakness in the investigation or to suggest further lines of inquiry. Of course, this will give the police an opportunity to tighten up their conclusions, but it will also give the defence a much better chance of persuading the police of the validity of the suspect's position. Provided that the exchange is conducted conscientiously and in good faith, there is nothing wrong in the police trying to make their case immune to defence objections, any more than it is wrong for the defence to knock holes into it.

This feature of the scheme might give rise to the objection that it would rarely be in the defence's interest to entrust the police with any exculpatory evidence or explanations lest the police try to make their case immune to any contradictory material. However, if taken to its logical conclusion, this consideration should lead defence lawyers to adopt a policy of general non-cooperation, of always invoking the right to maintain silence. Yet most suspect, even taking into account those who have access to legal advice, submit to interrogation, during which they reveal their exculpatory explanations. In other words, the police already have the opportunity to work out a refutation of exculpatory explanations. There is no reason why the suspect should not gain some benefit from waiver of the privilege of non-cooperation.

Eliminating the cat-and-mouse atmosphere

There is a further and more important point to be made here. The mutual suspicion engendered by the criminal process is a product of the present system, whereby the police and the suspect play cat and mouse with each other throughout the criminal process. The police have a right, and indeed the power, to question the suspect, while the suspect has the right, though not always an effective one, to suppress and conceal. But these tactics can be disadvantageous.

The suspect has a right to take no active part in the criminal investigation, or indeed in the rest of the criminal process. But non-participation is not necessarily a soft option, because it means that the field is left free to the police, and to some extent to the prosecution. It is they who construct the picture of reality on which the accused will be judged. This edifice is not built of pure objective fact, nor does it render a purely factual reality. It is not, as it were, an accurate, disinterested snapshot of a past event. No such thing exists. It is an account of a possible reality in which fact, imagination, and inference all play a part. Moreover, in an atmosphere of sharp adversity it is quite unrealistic to expect the police, or any other official, to aim at constructing possible accounts of innocence as well as of guilt. When we consider how criminal investigations are conducted, the protestations that the duty of the police and the prosecution is to unearth evidence of innocence as well as of guilt sound hollow. The questions which must be faced are: Is it sensible to leave the compilation of the account of the suspect's culpability entirely in the hands of the police? Would it not be sensible to devise some means by which the suspect could participate, on a less unequal footing than at present, in fashioning the story that is going to determine his or her fate?

A scheme under which the suspect and his or her solicitor could participate in the investigation would obviate the need to ban comment on the suspect's refusal to cooperate with the police. As we have seen, the sole reason that the Royal Commission gave for the maintenance of the ban was that the prospect of comment on refusal to answer questions might lead to pressure which could, in turn, produce false confessions (1993, pp. 49–55). Such pressure will be avoided in the scheme proposed here. However, it would be essential to the operation of such a scheme that all suspects are given legal advice. Since cost can be a serious constraint,[3] the scheme could be tried first in relation to serious offences.

Curtailment of the right to silence: the benefits

Legislation is now before Parliament to curtail the right to silence. The proposal is that comment on the suspect's failure to put forward a defence during the interrogation should be allowable at the trial and the caution would be changed accordingly. I have long maintained that there is little to support the privilege against self-incrimination and its offshoot, the right to silence (Zuckerman 1989, ch. 15). However, while the right to silence has little to commend itself, it does not follow that it may be fairly abolished without introducing adequate countervailing measures.

One of the reasons, we may speculate, that encouraged the government to curtail the right to silence, without adequate provision for the interests of suspects, was the feeble support given to the right by the Royal Commission. As we have seen, the Commission put forward one reason in support of the *status quo*. The Commission believed that a warning, telling suspects that failure to put forward their defence would count against them at the trial, would place extra pressure on suspects to confess. However, since, as things stand, the great majority of suspects make statements in the interrogation, the curtailment of the right of silence could make little difference in this regard. The supporters of curtailment would have been able to reason that since pressure which leads to statements in the majority of the cases gives, by implication from the report, no cause for concern, a little extra pressure should not make a great deal of difference, especially as such pressure would affect only those who have the fortitude to assert the right to silence and who are therefore less likely to be affected by pressure.

There is nothing inherently wrong with requiring a suspect to answer the police suspicions during the interrogation. But there is a lot wrong in expecting

---

[3]The Royal Commission thought that the prospect for a scheme of solicitors always being on duty at police stations was remote.

a suspect to do so in a process which lacks the most fundamental ingredient of fairness: information about the case to be answered. In no other legal procedure practised in this country is a person asked to put forward a defence to a claim without first being given a full and adequate account of the case against him or her. Being informed of the case against one is a fundamental prerequisite of procedural justice.

By forcing the suspect, in practice if not in theory, to defend him or herself without full knowledge of the case against him or her, the legislation will not only undermine procedural fairness, but will also create wide scope for police abuse. As the suspect and solicitor will be ignorant of the case that the police have against the suspect, the police will be able to tailor their case to the suspect's answer. We will have, to use a current phrase, interrogation by ambush. Yet, just as it is unfair to expect the prosecution to present their case at the trial in ignorance of the nature of the defence, so it is unfair to the suspect that he or she should have to answer the police case without knowledge of what that case really involves. It is no answer to say that procedural fairness is a requirement of legal proceedings, not of police interrogation. This would be a facetious argument given the extent to which the results of the police investigation influence the outcome of the trial. There can be no fair trial without fairness in the police station. Just as the admission of an improperly obtained confession affects the fairness of the trial so may the results of unfair questioning, once admitted in evidence, contaminate the fairness of the trial.

These arguments are not put forward in favour of the retention of the right to silence. They are put forward in favour of balancing the curtailment of that right with adequate procedural safeguards. The proposals put forward in the previous section would provide such safeguards.

However, it might not be necessary to wait upon the legislature to introduce a procedural counterbalance to the new caution and its threat of adverse comment. When a suspect is cautioned that, unless his or her excuses are mentioned during police questioning, the credibility of the suspect's defence at the trial would be undermined, the suspect is free to tell the police something along the following lines:

> I am prepared to answer your questions, but, in fairness, you should tell me first what case you have against me which requires an answer. It is reasonable to expect me to explain or excuse my conduct only when I am informed of the nature of the evidence that gives rise to suspicion concerning my conduct.

Should the police refuse to provide what the suspect, on advice from his or her solicitor, regards as fair notice of the nature of the police evidence and the suspect maintains silence, then, at the trial, the defence could apply for the evidence of the suspect's silence to be excluded under s. 78 of PACE. Under this section the judge may 'refuse to allow evidence on which the prosecution proposes to rely to be given if it appears to the court that, having regard to all the circumstances, the admission of the evidence would have such an adverse effect on the fairness of the proceedings that the court ought not to admit it'. The questioning of a suspect should be considered unfair, if the police have taken advantage of the suspect's ignorance by keeping him or her in the dark about the allegations and the evidence that the police had in their possession. Where the judge has refused to exclude evidence of silence, the suspect's request for information would have to be brought to the attention of the jury alongside his or her silence. If the jury can be convinced of the fairness of the demand for information, the adverse comment on the suspect's silence might be blunted and his or her silence would be less likely to count against him or her.

The judicial duty of ensuring a fair trial will place a burden on the judiciary to see to it that the use of silence in evidence does not undermine the fairness of the criminal process. This could have wide ranging consequences. For once parameters of fairness in interrogation are evolved for the purpose of determining the significance of silence, they would have to be applied generally and not just to those suspects who maintain silence. Thus, the abolition of the right of silence could lead to fairer interrogation procedures across the board. Unlike the right of silence, which offers some protection to those with the strength and determination to assert it, parameters of fairness would serve the interests of all suspects.

Conclusion

Although the criminal trial has great constitutional importance, it is not an effective and efficient instrument for discovering the truth since so much turns on the quality and reliability of the case prepared by the police and the prosecution. The trial is an examination of the police investigation; it is not itself an investigation of the crime. The trial can probe some aspects of the criminal investigation, but it cannot examine every aspect. The police investigation is bound to remain the foundation of the criminal process. Prosecutors who build their case on it will continue, by and large, to assume that it is sound, if only because once the foundation is laid its soundness is not easy to test. By the time a case reaches trial too much institutional capital has been invested in the assumption of guilt to allow for any further open-minded consideration of alternative hypotheses by those who have committed themselves to the prosecution. On their part, the courts are hampered in the assessment of the case for the prosecution by the assumption of police integrity and by the impracticability of examining all aspects of the investigation.

Clearly, it is far less efficient to try to correct flaws in a product already processed than to attempt to prevent them in the first place.

The report of the Royal Commission on Criminal Justice reflects the trial-oriented culture, and neglects the problematic nature of the case constructed by the police. The improvements recommended may prevent some of the more outrageous practices, but they only marginally address the real problems faced in the investigation of crime: bias and suggestibility. These are subtle factors. Their distorting influence is present even in the most congenial and civilised conditions of scientific research. They can be neutralised only through stringent and sophisticated procedures designed specifically for the purpose. The idea that by simply getting a better account of what has happened to the suspect in the police station we are going to improve the product of police investigation is wholly illusory.

A more promising way forward is through greater cooperation between the police and the suspect's legal representatives. It should be possible to devise a system by which the suspect's lawyer can make some contribution to counteract the effects of bias and of suggestibility. The system advocated in this chapter involves a gradual, progressive and mutual exchange of information between the suspect and his or her legal representatives, on the one side, and the police, on the other side. Curtailment of the right of silence would take us a step closer to such a solution, in that it would place pressure on the suspect to disclose his or her defence during the interrogation. However, the proposed abolition of the right to silence is lopsided and seriously unfair. For it forces the suspect to make a defence in ignorance of the case that the police have against him or her. It is a matter of the most fundamental fairness that a person who has to answer a charge should be given adequate information about that charge. Until adequate provision is made for supplying suspects with such information the process will not only be unfair, but also dangerous, because it creates considerable scope for abuse. However, the courts have ample jurisdiction to ensure that comment on silence is allowed only where the questioning of the suspect has been fair. Once the courts have evolved parameters of fairness, they would benefit not only the suspects who maintain silence but all suspects questioned by the police.

Whatever might be thought of the proposals put forward in this chapter, it seems clear that we have more or less reached the limits of the present strategy of checks and balances. In England today police powers are more effectively circumscribed than ever before, the interrogation and treatment of suspects are more closely monitored. But these measures are insufficient because they do not address the principal causes of miscarriage of justice: police bias and suspect and witness suggestibilty. To obtain a meaningful and lasting improvement in the administrtion of justice, we have to concentrate our efforts

139

on overcoming these cognitive obstacles and on obtaining a real improvement in the quality of police investigations.

References

Rosenthal, R. (1969), 'Interpersonal expectations: effects of the experimenter's hypothesis', in R. Rosenthal and R.L. Rosnow (eds), *Artifact in Behavioral Research* (New York and London).

Royal Commission on Criminal Justice (1993), *Report* (Cm 2263) (London: HMSO).

Royal Commission on Criminal Procedure (1981), *Report* (Cmnd 8092) (London: HMSO).

Zuckerman, A.A.S. (1989), *The Principles of Criminal Evidence* (London: Oxford University Press).

Zuckerman, A.A.S. (1992), 'Miscarriage of justice — a root treatment', *Criminal Law Review*, 323.

9

Abolition of the Right to Silence, 1972–1994

Michael Zander

The debate over the right to silence has now been raging for over 20 years since the Criminal Law Revision Committee (CLRC) (1972) proposed its abolition. There is often misunderstanding as to what is meant by proposals to abolish the right to silence. It has never in fact been suggested that silence itself should be prohibited. Abolition of the right to silence means rather giving the prosecution and the judge the right to invite the jury to draw adverse inferences from the accused's silence in the face of questioning by the police and at the trial.

The CLRC was a standing committee advisory to the Home Secretary. It consisted solely of lawyers — judges, barristers, solicitors and academics. It took no evidence before it produced its report, and it commissioned no research. Its recommendation was that failure during police questioning to mention any fact on which the accused subsequently relied at his or her trial could be made the subject of adverse comment by the prosecution and the court, and adverse inferences could be drawn against the accused from such silence. The accused would still have the right to be silent, but would exercise it at the risk that adverse inferences might be drawn if the jury (or the magistrates) thought that it would have been reasonable to expect the accused to have mentioned the facts in question while being questioned. This would apply not only to facts raised in the accused's evidence but equally to facts referred to in the evidence of other witnesses:

> To forbid it seems to us to be contrary to common sense and, without helping the innocent, to give an unnecessary advantage to the guilty. Hardened criminals often take advantage of the present rule to refuse to answer any

questions at all, and this may greatly hamper the police and even bring their investigations to a halt. Therefore the abolition of the restriction would help justice. (Criminal Law Revision Committee 1972, para. 30.)

The recommendation was unanimous. The CLRC likewise proposed that adverse inferences could be drawn in respect of the accused's refusal to give evidence at the trial. Both proposals ran into such a storm of criticism that the entire report had to be shelved at the time (Zander 1974).

The issue was next considered by the Royal Commission on Criminal Procedure (1981), which, by a majority, rejected the view of the CLRC. If adverse inferences could be drawn from the fact of silence it might 'put strong (and additional) psychological pressure upon some suspects to answer questions without knowing precisely what was the substance of and evidence for the accusations against them' (Royal Commission on Criminal Procedure 1981, para. 4.50). This, in the Commission's view, 'might well increase the risk of innocent people, particularly those under suspicion for the first time, making damaging statements' (ibid., loc. cit.). Moreover, they suggested, 'to use a suspect's silence as evidence against him seems to run counter to a central element in the accusatorial system at trial' (1981, para. 4.41). There was an inconsistency of principle 'in requiring the onus of proof at trial to be upon the prosecution and to be discharged without any assistance from the accused, and yet in enabling the prosecution to use the accused's silence in the face of police questioning under caution as any part of the case against him at trial' (ibid., loc. cit.).

The Conservative government which implemented the Royal Commission's report in the Police and Criminal Evidence Act 1984 (PACE) accepted the Commission's recommendation that the right to silence be preserved. The Bill was first introduced by Mr William Whitelaw. After the general election of May 1983 had interrupted the Bill's progress, it was reintroduced after the election by the new Home Secretary, Mr Leon Brittan. During the debates on PACE neither Mr Whitelaw nor Mr Brittan so much as suggested any discontent with the proposed preservation of the right to silence. PACE came into force as from 1 January 1986.

But only 18 months later, in July 1987, the then Home Secretary, Mr Douglas Hurd, unexpectedly reopened the whole issue. Delivering the annual Police Foundation lecture, he affirmed his belief in the appropriateness of giving suspects access to legal advice in the police station. He continued:

However, in the light of changing circumstances, including the advent of tape recording and other safeguards, it is right to consider whether the right balance is being struck between the interests of a person suspected of crime and the interests of society as a whole in bringing criminals to justice.... Is it really in the interests of justice, for example, that experienced criminals should be able to refuse to answer all police questions secure in the knowledge that a jury will never hear of it?[1] Does the present law really protect the innocent whose interests will generally lie in answering questions frankly? Is it really unthinkable that the jury should be allowed to know about the defendant's silence and, in the light of the other facts brought to light during a trial, be able to draw its own conclusions? I shall not seek to provide answers now. But I think these are questions which informed public opinion might address over the coming weeks.

The Royal Commission on Criminal Procedure had been at pains to demonstrate that their report represented a fair balance between the interests of the suspect and of the police. This concept of balance had been referred to repeatedly by the ministers steering PACE through Parliament. Without suggesting that there were any new facts, Mr Hurd was seemingly prepared to upset this carefully constructed balance. He called for a public debate on an issue on which there had been extensive debate during the previous 15 years — and which had seemingly been settled.

Further debate duly ensued. But less than a year later Mr Hurd seemed virtually to have made up his mind. On 18 May 1988 in a written Parliamentary answer Mr Hurd said that, having listed to the arguments for and against change:

> I am not convinced that the protection which the law now gives to the accused person who ambushes the prosecution can be justified. The case for change is strong.... But I am persuaded by some of the comments that have been made that more careful work needs to be done before we can bring forward with confidence a specific proposal for legislation. (Parliamentary Debates (Hansard), Commons, 6th ser., vol. 133, written answers, cols 465-6, 18 May 1988.)

He announced the setting up of a Home Office Working Group[2] to consider, not whether the right of silence should be abolished, but 'the precise form of the change in the law which would best achieve our purpose'.

---

[1] The Home Secretary was mistaken — the jury does normally learn from the evidence that the suspect was silent in the face of police questioning (see Zander and Henderson 1993, p. 7, para. 1.2.5).

[2] The chairman was W.J. Bohan of the Home Office. The members were K.R. Ashken of the Crown Prosecution Service; C.F. Bailey, Assistant Chief Constable of West Yorkshire; B.A. Blackwell of the Northern Ireland Office; Michael Kalisher QC; and a practising solicitor, Mr P.M. Raphael.

But before the working group's report was published, the right to silence had been abolished *for all offences* in Northern Ireland. This happened in the form of an Order laid before the House of Commons in draft in October 1988 by the Secretary of State for Northern Ireland, Mr Tom King. A draft order laid in that way cannot be amended in Parliament — it can only be debated. The draft Criminal Evidence (Northern Ireland) Order 1988 was approved in Parliament, then made on November 14 and it came into force one month later.[3]

The Home Office working group's report (1989) was published in July 1989. (For discussion of the differences between the recommendations of the CLRC's 1972 report and the recommendations of the Home Office working group see Zander 1993 and chapter 1 above.) Commenting on the report, the Home Secretary, Mr Hurd, was quoted in a Home Office press handout as saying:

> Today's report offers one way of reducing the scope for unfair exploitation by a suspect of his right to decline to answer questions from the police or to give evidence in court. Before reaching a final view, the government want to hear what others have to say, and to take account of the effectiveness of the 1988 Northern Ireland Criminal Evidence Order.[4]

Informed observers assumed that the government would include provisions to give effect to the working group's proposals in the next Criminal Justice Bill. In the event this did not happen, probably because the atmosphere was being increasingly soured by the implications of the three IRA miscarriage of justice cases — the cases of the Guildford Four, the Maguires and the Birmingham Six. In the light of the concerns aroused by those cases, it probably did not seem a propitious time to abolish the right to silence.

The Royal Commission on Criminal Justice, the establishment of which was announced by the Prime Minister on the day that the Birmingham Six had their

---

[3] For the Parliamentary debates see Parliamentary Debates (Hansard), Commons, 6th ser., vol. 140, cols 184–225, 8 November 1988; Lords, 5th ser., vol. 501, cols 774–803, 10 November 1988.

[4] There has not as yet been any published review of the Northern Ireland experience. The Royal Commission on Criminal Justice received a study entitled 'An examination of the "right of silence" in Northern Ireland' prepared by an inspector in the Crime Department of the Royal Ulster Constabulary as part of an honours degree course. The study, running to some 80 pages, was based on the recorded behaviour of almost 500 suspects during 768 interviews. It was forwarded to the Royal Commission by Mr W.G. Monahan, Assistant Chief Constable of the RUC. The study has not been published and it was not referred to by the Royal Commission in their report. I asked Mr Monahan for permission to cite from the report but, to my regret, this permission was refused without explanation.

Commenting in *The Guardian* on 8 March 1994 on the absence of information about the Northern Ireland experience, Owen Bowcott said: 'No statistics have been trumpeted to suggest an increased conviction rate. No ministers have bragged about break throughs in their campaigns against paramilitaries. It is an awkward silence from which some have already begun to draw adverse inferences.' See also JUSTICE, 1994.

convictions quashed, was specifically asked to look at the question of the right to silence.[5] The Commission, by a majority of eight to three, preferred the view of their predecessors, the Royal Commission on Criminal Procedure, to that of the CLRC. The chief reason they gave was concern that abolition of the right of silence would increase the risk of miscarriages of justice:

> The majority of us, however, believe that the possibility of an increase in the convictions of the guilty is outweighed by the risk that the extra pressure on suspects to talk in the police station and the adverse inferences invited if they do not may result in more convictions of the innocent. (Royal Commission on Criminal Justice 1993, p. 54, para. 22.)

But the Home Secretary, Mr Michael Howard, decided to reject the advice of the Royal Commission. He chose the Conservative Party's annual conference on 6 October 1993 to make the announcement:

> As I talk to people up and down the country, there is one part of our law in particular that makes their blood boil. I haven't yet mentioned it. It's the so-called right of silence. This is of course a complete misnomer. What is at stake is not the right to refuse to answer questions. But if a suspect does remain silent should the prosecution and the judge or magistrate be allowed to comment on it? Should they have the right to take it into account in deciding guilt or innocence?
>
> The so-called right to silence is ruthlessly exploited by terrorists. What fools they must think we are. It's time to call a halt to this charade. The so-called right to silence will be abolished.[6]

In summary, the government's decision to abolish the right to silence in the Criminal Justice and Public Order Bill introduced in December 1993 was a belated implementation of the CLRC's 1972 report (in the form adopted in Northern Ireland) in defiance of the view of two Royal Commissions.

In my view, this decision of the government verges on the unconstitutional. Governments of course generally have the right, and indeed the duty, to decide whether to implement the proposals of advisory bodies whether they be

---

[5] Its terms of reference asked the Commission to consider, *inter alia*: '(v) the opportunities available for an accused person to state his position on the matters charged and the extent to which the courts might draw adverse inferences from primary facts, the conduct of the accused, and any failure on his part to take advantage of an opportunity to state his position.'

[6] For Mr Howard's statement in support of the proposed abolition of the right to silence on the second-reading debate see Parliamentary Debates (Hansard), Commons, 6th ser., vol. 235, cols 26–8, 11 January 1994. For Mr Howard's explanations of the government's amendments to its Bill regarding the right to silence see ibid., vol. 241, cols 276–81, 13 April 1994.

standing bodies like the Law Commission or the CLRC, or *ad hoc* bodies such as Royal Commissions or departmental committees. There is therefore no objection in principle to a government rejecting the view of a Royal Commission. However, this matter is I think exceptional. The issue is one of fundamental principle on which opinion is sharply divided. It is therefore quintessentially the kind of issue on which the view of a Royal Commission is valuable. The government plainly acknowledged this fact by specifically including the question in the terms of reference given to the Royal Commission on Criminal Justice. That Commission took extensive evidence on the subject and considered all the extant research in depth. It deliberated on the matter at length. Its view was that of a clear majority — eight out of 11 commissioners. So far as I am aware, no new significant facts were available to the Home Secretary after the Commission reported.[7] The Home Secretary's decision to reject the Commission's advice was, I believe, based essentially on nothing more substantial than his view, backed by his cabinet colleagues, that he preferred the opinion of the minority.

I do not suggest that abolition of the right to silence is supported only by police officers and Conservative cabinet ministers. As has been seen, it was first proposed by the CLRC, an extremely reputable body, albeit one consisting only of judges and lawyers. It is supported by great numbers of judges[8] and no doubt by many members of the public. But the matter having (rightly) been put to the Royal Commission on Criminal Justice which had the opportunity of considering the issue in depth, I regard the government's decision to override the view of the Commission as a debasement of the process of public decision-making. The right to silence is no trivial issue. Both its champions and its critics agree that the right to silence is a matter of real constitutional importance.[9] For party politicians to prefer their own opinions on so important a matter of principle to that of two Royal Commissions, one of which was specifically asked its advice on the matter, where the government has no new arguments nor any better basis of judgment is in my view deplorable.

To listen to the protagonists in the debate over the right to silence one might think that there was serious disagreement over the relevant facts. My own

---

[7] If the ACPO survey (1993) referred to by Roger Leng in chapter 1 (p. 23 above) was considered to be significant, it should be noted that it was produced *after* the Home Secretary announced at the Conservative Party conference on 6 October that the right to silence was to be abolished. The study was based on data collected in September 1993. It was announced in the press on 1 December 1993. For details see Neyroud 1994.

[8] The Lord Chief Justice, Lord Taylor of Gosforth expressed his view in a lecture (1994) supporting abolition of the right to silence but criticising the provision in the Bill that judges would be required to ask the defendant to step into the witness-box. The government eventually dropped this clause, see Parliamentary Debates (Hansard), Commons, 6th ser., vol. 241, col. 280, 13 April 1994.

[9] The Home Secretary, Mr Michael Howard, said on the Report Stage of the Bill 'I certainly accept that the matter ... is of considerable constitutional significance' (Parliamentary Debates (Hansard), Commons, 6th ser., vol. 241, col. 276, 13 April 1994).

assessment is that many of the relevant facts are now sufficiently well-established and that what is in dispute is mainly what they signify or what facts are most relevant.

Research results and general statistics of the criminal justice system appears to establish that:

(a)   The great majority of suspects in police stations do not exercise their right to silence. All studies agree on this.

(b)   Suspects charged with serious offences are silent in the police station more often than suspects charged with less serious cases. See Moston et al. 1992, table 9. The study by Moston et al. distinguished between three categories of case from the point of view of 'silence' — those who made admissions, those who denied the charges and those who neither admitted nor denied the charges. The third category are treated for present purposes as having exercised their right to silence. See also Moston et al 1993, p 37, table 3; ACPO 1993.

(c)   Suspects who have legal advice are more likely to be silent in the police station than suspects who do not have legal advice.

Different studies have produced very different relative figures. At one extreme Sanders et al. (1989, p. 135) in their study for the Lord Chancellor's Department found that 2% of 527 suspects were silent and that when they had legal advisers present the proportion rose to 7%.

The study of 1,067 cases by Moston et al. (1992, table 10) showed 'use of the right of silence' by 26% of suspects who had had legal advice compared with 10% of those who had not had legal advice. When legal advice was correlated with strength of evidence, there was no difference when the evidence was weak. When the evidence was strong, nearly 80% of those without legal advice admitted the offence, compared with only 49% of those who had legal advice. Those who had legal advice denied the offence (23%) or neither admitted nor denied (28%). (Moston et al. 1992, p. 36.)

In the ACPO study (1993) of 3,633 cases, 57% of suspects who had legal advice exercised the right to silence, compared with 13% of those who did not have legal advice.

It is worth noting that only some 30% of suspects have legal advice in the police station either in person or over the telephone — see Annual Reports of the Legal Aid Board.

(d)   Suspects with previous convictions are more likely to be silent in the police station than those with no prior record. See Moston et al. 1993, p. 38, table 4. See also Moston et al. 1992, pp. 36–7, which gives the correlation between criminal record and strength of evidence. With increasing strength of evidence, admissions rose steadily. But the rate at which they rose was affected by whether or not the accused had a prior record. Thus when there was strong evidence and the suspect had a criminal record, about 21% of suspects declined to comment on an accusation, compared with approximately 11% of suspects without a criminal record.

(e) What determines whether a suspect is charged is mainly the strength of the prosecution's evidence. See Moston et al. 1993, p. 42. When the evidence was weak, only about 23% of suspects were charged; with moderately strong evidence about 63% were charged and with strong evidence nearly 92% were charged.

(f) Insofar as silence in the police station has any impact on the police decision to charge, it makes a charge more rather than less likely. See Moston et al. 1993, tables 8 and 9: 'Use of silence as such had no statistical effect on the decision to charge or release suspects' (pp. 42–3). Where the evidence was weak the suspect was normally not charged, regardless of whether he was silent or not. Where the evidence was strong, he normally was charged regardless of whether he had been silent. But where the evidence was neither weak nor strong, the police charged in 58% of cases where the suspect had been silent — compared with 45% of cases where he had denied the allegation (p. 43).

(g) The great majority of defendants in both the Crown Court (over 70%) and the magistrates' courts (over 90%) plead guilty, which from this point of view makes it academic whether they were silent in the police station. A high proportion of suspects who are silent in the police station end by pleading guilty. The study by Moston et al. (1993, p. 46) showed that suspects who were silent in the police station were actually *more* likely to plead guilty than those who had not — 67% compared with 49% in a matched sample who were not silent.

(h) Suspects who are silent in the police station and who plead not guilty are found guilty about as often as suspects who were not silent in the police station. The study by Moston et al. (1993, p. 46) stated that 80% of the silence group were found guilty compared with 77% of the control group.

What is in dispute is whether, and if so, in what way, 'abolition of the right to silence' would affect the proportion of suspects who (a) are silent in the police station; (b) are silent in the police station and are not charged; and (c) are silent in the police station, are charged and are not convicted. My own best estimate on all three questions is that the effect of abolition of the right to silence will be negligible. I am especially sceptical whether the police will gain much advantage in the serious cases that give most reason for concern. Defendants in serious cases who are silent today will probably still be silent because their experience of the criminal justice system will suggest to them that the value of silence is likely greatly to outweigh the penalty of adverse inferences. Both the Royal Commissions took this view. The Royal Commission on Criminal Procedure said (1981, para. 4.50):

> The guilty person who knew the system would be inclined to sit it out. If his arrest had been on reasonable suspicion only and this were not enough to make a prima facie case, he would lose nothing and gain everything by keeping silent, since he would not be prosecuted if no other evidence emerged.

Even where the police did have solid evidence it might be worthwhile, the Commission suggested, for the suspect to remain silent and produce his defence at a late stage in the hope that it might be beileved by the jury (ibid., loc. cit.).

The Royal Commission on Criminal Justice said (1993, p. 54, para. 22) that the majority who favoured retention of the right to silence doubted whether its abolition would have the effect the police supposed:

> The experienced professional criminals who wish to remain silent are likely to continue to do so and will justify their silence by stating at trial that their solicitors have advised them to say nothing at least until the allegations against them have been fully disclosed.

Juries can already draw adverse inferences from the fact that the defendant was silent. How much difference would the prosecution and the judge's invitation to draw such adverse inferences make? I imagine that the word amongst streetwise professional criminals will be that the change in the law makes no difference to recommended behaviour in the police station.

The unknown quantity will be what streetwise solicitors advise clients. At present, solicitors and their staffs vary greatly in the advice they give. The new training kit on police station skills issued by the Law Society in March 1994 states that there may be many different reasons for counselling the client not to answer police questions. Thus 'if the prosecution evidence is not likely to be sufficient to charge or convict your client (or you have inadequate information to make this assessment) then you should strongly advise your client against helping the prosecution to make a case by answering police questions' (Shepherd 1994, p. 172).

Exercising the right to silence had 'other definite defence advantages'. It enabled the defence to 'listen to and further evaluate the strengths and weaknesses of the prosecution case in terms of the extent and quality of the police investigation ... the sufficiency of the evidence, the strength of the evidence, the investigating officer's awareness of and attitude towards the reliability of information and its source' (ibid., loc. cit.). Silence also protected the client from conversation and questioning which might induce him or her to confess just to stop the interview, 'to get out of the room and out of police detention' or where, because of 'confusion, doubt and distrust of his or her memory' the client came to believe he or she was guilty when this was not the case (ibid., loc. cit.). It also avoided discussion of any earlier confession which might have been obtained improperly. Finally it conserved the client's mental and physical resources. The new guide says that exercise of the right of silence 'must be consistent' (ibid., p. 173) and indicates that it is hard to maintain: 'it needs grit, doggedness, self-control and single-mindedness' (ibid., loc. cit.).

But what difference would the abolition of the right to silence make? The guide refers to the fact that the government had announced its intention to abolish the right to silence. It continues:

> You should not be panicked into thinking that a change [in regard to the right to silence] would mean that you would have to adopt a completely different approach to formulating your advice to a client. *In practical terms, such a change would actually make little difference to the advice you give.* (Emphasis added.)

From a police point of view this is less than encouraging. The guide continues that it could be argued that if the client remained silent the risk of being wrongfully convicted might well be *less* than the risk of being wrongfully convicted if the client talked to the police. Talking to the police would pose a *greater risk* of wrongful conviction if, for example, the client was 'in an emotional, highly compliant and highly suggestible state of mind at the time of the interview', or was 'confused and liable to make mistakes which could be interpreted — incorrectly — as deliberate lies at any subsequent trial', or if the client 'forgot important details, distrusted his or her memory ... went along with [police] suggestive questioning and as a result damaged his or her case in court', or 'used loose expressions, unaware of the possible adverse interpretations which could be placed upon them at trial', or there was some other reason why he or she might 'perform badly during the interview' (ibid., pp. 181–2).

The guide suggests that a judge should not allow comment on the suspect's silence when there is an innocent explanation for it. Examples of innocent explanations would be where the suspect wanted to protect others, where he or she wanted to conceal something discreditable, indiscreet or embarrassing, and where the prosecution had not sufficiently revealed the police case. Another example of an innocent explanation for silence, the guide suggests, would be where the legal adviser quite properly used the suspect's silence in order to prize information about the prosecution's case from the police (ibid., p. 184).

In addition to all the reasons mentioned by the Law Society's (excellent) new guide there is another valid reason for advising a client to be silent. This is the inexperience of the adviser. Research has established that most legal advice in police stations is given by persons who are not qualified solicitors (Zander and Henderson 1993, p. 194; McConville et al. 1994, p. 84). It is also clear that much of such advice is given at present by persons who do not have the necessary skills (McConville et al. 1994, pp. 83–90 and 104–8; Hodgson and McConville 1993). It is precisely for that reason that the Law Society has issued its new kit and guide to improve police station advisory skills (Ames 1994) and the Legal Aid Board has stated that as from February 1995 payment will not be given for advice given in police stations by clerks unless they have passed the new accreditation test which will apply to all persons except trainee solicitors and authorised duty solicitors (McLeod 1993). This new rule and the Law Society's new 1,000-page training kit represent a major step in the right direction. But even in the best of all possible future worlds it is inevitable that legal advisers in police stations will continue to vary in terms of experience and ability. The less experienced and the less able the adviser, the more likely it is that he or she will adopt a play-safe strategy of counselling the client to be silent.

It is entirely possible therefore that advice to be silent will continue much as before. But there is another possibility, which from a police point of view is considerably worse — that abolition of the right to silence will make solicitors *more* rather than less likely to advise the client to be silent. The reason is that if a suspect is silent on the basis of legal advice it can be put to the jury that no adverse inference should be drawn. How can the suspect be blamed if all he or she did was to act on professional advice? This is what has happened in Scotland in regard to judicial examination. Judicial examination was introduced by the Criminal Justice (Scotland) Act 1980 on the recommendation of the Thomson Committee Report. The Committee saw it as a way to give the accused 'at the earliest possible stage in the judicial process an opportunity of stating his position as regards the charge against him'. The jury would be allowed to draw adverse inferences from 'the accused's failure to disclose at judicial examination a particular line of defence on which he relies at trial' (Committee on Criminal Procedure in Scotland 1975, pp. 39–48). But in the event this innovation proved to be useless. Defence lawyers generally advised clients to say nothing at the judicial examination and judges have accepted that in these circumstances juries cannot draw adverse inferences from silence. (The Royal Commission on Criminal Justice stated: 'This, we understand, is what has effectively happened in Scotland where the accused routinely decline to comment on the charges against them at a preliminary hearing, known as a judicial examination, before a judge (1993, p. 54, n. 9).) The same is likely to happen here.

The net effect therefore is that abolition of the right to silence is likely to make little, if any, useful contribution to successful prosecutions and may even make matters worse for the prosecution. It is also bound to lead to much legal argument about the circumstances in which adverse inferences can be drawn. The suspect was silent when first arrested and was then silent at the police station after receiving legal advice. If the prosecution cannot invite the jury to draw adverse inferences from silence after legal advice, can they suggest that adverse inferences can be drawn from silence on arrest before any legal advice was given? Can adverse inferences be drawn from silence even though the police questions did not allude to the matter in issue. Is a suspect who is not questioned at all to be penalised for not volunteering facts on which he or she later relies at trial? How is the suspect supposed to know what he or she should say at that stage? It is predictable that the area will become a legal minefield. As Roger Leng has pointed out (chapter 1 above), it will also have the unfortunate effect of placing more emphasis on exchanges (or alleged exchanges) outside the police station. Pre-PACE there was much heated controversy over 'verballing' when words were said to have been put into the mouth of the suspect by police officers. Are we now to have 'non-verballing', where defendants claim that they are falsely alleged to have been silent in response to questions that either were not asked or to which they did in fact reply?

The impact of such a change on juries is of course unpredictable. The Royal Commission on Criminal Justice proposed that the Contempt of Court Act 1981, s. 8, should be amended so as to permit authorised research in jury rooms. The first Interim Response to the Report stated that 'The government is sympathetic to the Commission's recommendation that the law should be amended so as to allow research to be conducted into the reasons for jury verdicts; but it is still considering the precise scope of the research that the law might allow and the rules under which it might be carried out' (Home Office 1994, para. 12). If this were to come to pass, it could be of great interest.

In the meanwhile we can only speculate what juries make of an accused's silence. In the Crown Court study done for the Royal Commission we asked judges in cases where the evidence showed that the defendant had been silent in the police station, 'If you had been a member of the jury, how would you have interpreted the defendant's silence?' They were then offered three alternative answers: (a) 'probably adversely, the silence seemed suspicious', (b) 'probably not adversely, the silence was explicable' and (c) 'don't know'. There were 180 responses. In 41% the judges answered 'probably adversely', in 42% they answered 'probably not adversely', and in 17% they answered 'don't know' (Zander and Henderson 1993, p. 8). There was therefore no clear result — other than confirmation of the obvious point that silence is by no means necessarily to be taken as evidence of guilt.

Opinions vary as to the origins of the right to silence. The CLRC stated in its report that it did not fully emerge until the 19th century (1972, para. 21). A possibly more authoritative view is that of Wigmore who considered that it became part of the common law in the mid 17th century following the collapse of the political courts of Star Chamber and Commission which possessed the power to compel witnesses to testify under oath (Wigmore 1961, sect. 2250; for more references see Greer 1990, pp. 710–11; Wood and Crawford 1989). But, whether it is very ancient or a 19th-century development, there can be no doubt that the suspect's right to silence has for the whole of the modern period been an integral part of the system. Now, at the time of writing (June 1994) it seems as if within months it will have been unceremoniously dispatched.

Perhaps however this will not be the end of the story. A case challenging the abolition of the right to silence in Northern Ireland has been declared admissible by the European Commission of Human Rights. The case is that of *Murray* v *UK* involving conviction for terrorism offences in Northern Ireland.[10] It will take some years before the European Court of Human Rights rules on the issue. The court's recent case law suggests that the government cannot be entirely sanguine about the prospects.[11]

Thus in *Funke* v *France* (1993) 16 EHRR 297, the European Court of Human Rights held that the applicant's right to a fair trial under art. 6(1) of the Convention had been infringed by a requirement to disclose documents concerning his tax affairs that would incriminate him. He had been asked to supply documents regarding assets abroad to customs officers. When he refused, criminal proceedings were commenced for a fine and a daily penalty of 50 francs until such time as he produced the documents. (Because the European Court upheld his claim that this criminal conviction violated his right to a fair trial under art. 6(1), it did not give judgment on his claim that it also infringed his right to be presumed innocent until proved guilty under art. 6(2).) Funke argued that the criminal proceedings had been brought to compel him to cooperate in a prosecution brought against him. The French government argued that the customs authorities had not required Funke to confess to a crime or to provide evidence of one himself. They had merely asked him to give

---

[10]The defendant was charged in a Diplock court with attempted murder and possession of a firearm with intent to endanger life. At the close of the prosecution's case he elected not to give evidence and the judge thereupon directed himself that under the Criminal Evidence (Northern Ireland) Order 1988, art. 4, he was entitled to draw adverse inferences from the failure to give evidence. He convicted the defendant. The Court of Appeal and the House of Lords both dismissed his appeal — see *Murray* v *Director of Public Prosecutions* [1994] 1 WLR 1. For a discussion of the House of Lords decision see Jackson 1993.

[11]It was reported in April 1994 that three leading barristers (Roy Amlott QC, Richard Plender QC and Peter Duffy QC) had given JUSTICE an opinion that the government's right of silence proposals infringed article 6 of the European Convention. See *Solicitors' Journal*, vol. 138, 15 April, p. 355. Their view was based largely on the *Funke* case.

particulars of evidence found by their officers during a search of his home. The courts for their part had merely assessed whether the customs' application was justified.

The European Commission of Human Rights had found in favour of the French government. It considered that neither the obligation to produce bank statements not the imposition of pecuniary penalties offended the principle of a fair trial. The former was reasonable. Responsibility for the detriment caused by the latter lay entirely with the person affected when he refused to cooperate with the authorities.

In spite of these powerful considerations, the Court of Human Rights upheld the claim. The judgment on the point is frustratingly terse — running to just one brief paragraph of 10 lines. It said the criminal conviction was in order to obtain documents which the customs officers believed must exist:

> Being unable or unwilling to procure them by some other means, they attempted to compel the applicant himself to provide the evidence of offences he had allegedly committed. The special features of customs laws ... cannot justify such an infringement of the right of anyone 'charged with a criminal offence' within the autonomous meaning of this expression in article 6, to remain silent and not to contribute to incriminating himself.

There had accordingly been a breach of art. 6(1). See also two similar cases decided by the court on the same day: *Miailhe* v *France* (1993) 16 EHRR 332; *Cremieux* v *France* (1993) 16 EHRR 357.

It seems therefore that the Court *is* prepared to protect the right to silence. It would be poetic justice if the government's move to abolish the right to silence were held to be unlawful by the European Court of Human Rights.

References

ACPO (1993), *The Right of Silence: Briefing Paper* (London: Association of Chief Police Officers of England, Wales and Northern Ireland).

Ames, J. (1994), 'Boosting police station skills', *Law Society's Gazette*, vol. 91, No. 6, 9 February, p. 9.

Committee on Criminal Procedure in Scotland (1975), *Second Report* (Cmnd 6218) (London: HMSO).

Criminal Law Revision Committee (1972), *Eleventh Report: Evidence (General)* (Cmnd 4991) (London: HMSO).

Greer, S. (1990), 'The right to silence: a review of the current debate', *Modern Law Review*, vol. 53, p. 709.

Hodgson, J., and McConville, M. (1993), 'Silence and the suspect', *New Law Journal*, vol. 143, 7 May, p. 659.

Home Office (1989), *Report of the Working Group on the Right to Silence* (London: Home Office).

Home Office (1994), *Interim Government Response to the Report of the Royal Commission on Criminal Justice* (London: HMSO).

Jackson, J. (1993), 'Inferences from silence: from common law to common sense', *Northern Ireland Legal Quarterly*, vol. 44, pp. 103–12.

JUSTICE (1994), 'The Right to Silence Debate: The Northern Ireland Experience', May 1994.

McConville, M., et al. (1994), *Standing Accused* (Oxford: Clarendon Press).

McLeod, J. (1993), 'Alarm at end of right to silence', *Law Society's Gazette*, vol. 90, No. 38, p. 9.

Moston, S., Stephenson, G.M., and Williamson, T. (1992), 'The effects of case characteristics on suspect behaviour during questioning', *British Journal of Criminology*, vol. 32, pp. 23–40.

Moston, S., Stephenson, G.M., and Williamson, TM (1993), 'The incidence, antecedents and consequences of the use of the right to silence during police questioning', *Criminal Behaviour and Mental Health*, vol. 3, pp. 30–47.

Neyroud, P. (1994), 'Wrongs about a right', *Police Review* (8 April), pp. 17–20.

Royal Commission on Criminal Justice (1993), *Report* (Cmnd 2263) (London: HMSO).

Royal Commission on Criminal Procedure (1981), *Report* (Cmnd 8092) (London: HMSO).

Sanders, A., et al. (1989) *Advice and Assistance at Police Stations and the 24-Hour Duty Solicitor Scheme* (London: Lord Chancellor's Department).

Shepherd, E. (1994), *Becoming Skilled: A Resource Book*, in a pack of training materials entitled *Police Station Skills for Legal Advisers* (London: Law Society).

Taylor of Gosforth, Lord (1994), 'Tom Sargent memorial lecture', *New Law Journal*, vol. 144, 28 January, pp. 125–9.

Wigmore, J.H. (1961), *Evidence in Trials at Common Law*, vol. 8, revised by J.T. McNaughton (Boston MA: Little Brown).

Wood, J., and Crawford, A. (1989), *The Right of Silence* (Civil Liberties Trust).

Zander, M. (1974), 'The CLRC report — a survey of reactions', *Law Society's Gazette* (7 October).

Zander, M. (1993), 'How will the right of silence be abolished?', *New Law Journal*, vol. 143, 2 December, pp. 1716–18.

Zander, M., and Henderson, P. (1993), *The Crown Court Study* (Royal Commission on Criminal Justice Research Study No. 19) (London: HMSO).